HarperCollins Publishers
Westerhill Road
Bishopbriggs
Glasgow
G64 2QT

First Edition 2012

ISBN 978-0-00-745718-2

Reprint 10 9 8 7 6 5 4 3 2 1 0

© HarperCollins Publishers 2012

© 1976, 2012 Sanrio Co., Ltd

Collins® is a registered trademark of
HarperCollins Publishers Limited

www.collinslanguage.com

A catalogue record for this book is
available from the British Library

Printed in China by Imago

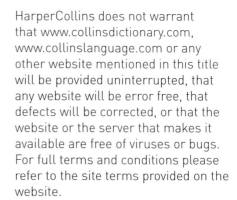

Design concept
Jemma Beal

Page design
Perfect Bound Ltd

Typesetting
Davidson Publishing Solutions, Glasgow

Editors
Sandra Anderson
Gerry Breslin
Elspeth Summers

For the publisher
Lucy Cooper
Julianna Dunn
Kerry Ferguson
Elaine Higgleton
Catherine Lutman

How to find a word in this dictionary

It is easy to use a dictionary if you know the alphabetical order of letters.

ate - axe

A

B
C
D
E
F
G
H
I
J
K
L
M
N
O

ate
💜 Look at **eat**
*My sister **ate** three biscuits at lunchtime.*

atlas *noun*
atlases
An **atlas** is a book of maps.

attack *verb*
attacks, attacking, attacked
If someone **attacks** another person, they try to hurt them.

attention *noun*
If you pay **attention**, you watch and listen.
*Hello Kitty always pays **attention** in class.*

attract *verb*
attracts, attracting, attracted
If something **attracts** things to it, it makes them move towards it.
*Magnets **attract** anything made of iron.*

J
K
L
M
N
O
P
Q

bright *adjective*
brighter, brightest
1 A **bright** colour is very easy to see.

*Hello Kitty wore a **bright** red dress.*
2 Something that is **bright** shines with a lot of light.
*The sun is very **bright** today.*

brilliant *adjective*
Something that is **brilliant** is very good.
*Hello Kitty thought the film was **brilliant**.*

1 Think of the first letter, and look at the side of the page to find the right pages in the dictionary.

2 Think of the second letter, and look at the words at the top of the page, to help you find the page you need.

3 Now look down the list of words on the page, to find the word you are looking for.

4 You can check how to spell words.

5 You can see how the word changes when it is used in different ways.

6 You can see what the word means.

7 You can see how the word is used in a sentence.

8 You can see if a word has more than one meaning.

9 You can see if a word is a noun, verb or adjective. Some words can be used in more than one way.

How words work

Nouns

Nouns are words that describe people, places or things.

> **arm** *noun*
> **bird** *noun*
> **car** *noun*

If you have more than one of the thing, you use the word that ends in **–S**.

> **arms**
> **birds**
> **cars**

Adjectives

Adjectives tell you what things, people or places are like.

> **happy** *adjective*
> **fast** *adjective*
> **wild** *adjective*

Adjectives can be used in different ways.

> **happier, happiest**
> **faster, fastest**
> **wilder, wildest**

Verbs

Verbs are words that describe the things that you do.

> **eat** *verb*
> **cry** *verb*
> **talk** *verb*

Verbs can be used in different ways.

> **eats, eating, ate, eaten**
> **cries, crying, cried**
> **talks, talking, talked**

Verbs can be used to talk about things that you are doing now.

*He **teaches** people how to play the piano.*
*Hello Kitty **thinks** it's a great idea.*

They can be used to talk about things that you did in the past.

*She **took** the plates into the kitchen.*
*She **talked** to him on the phone.*

They can also be used to talk about things that you will do in the future.

*Mum **will** be angry.*
***We'll** come along later.*

Aa

abacus *noun*
abacuses

An **abacus** is a frame with beads that move along pieces of wire. It is used for counting.

able

If you are **able** to do something, you know how to do it.
*Hello Kitty is **able** to swim.*

about

1 **About** means to do with.
*This book is **about** history.*

2 **About** also means near to something.
*His grandfather is **about** 80 years old.*

above

If something is **above** another thing, it is over it or higher than it.
*The balloon floated **above** his head.*

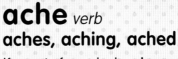

accident *noun*
accidents

1 An **accident** is something nasty that happens, and that hurts someone.
*He broke his leg in a car **accident**.*

2 If something happens by **accident**, you do not expect it to happen.
*Hello Kitty dropped a cup by **accident**.*

ache *verb*
aches, aching, ached

If a part of your body **aches**, you feel a steady pain there.
*My leg **aches** a lot.*

acorn *noun*
acorns

An **acorn** is the seed of an oak tree.

across

If someone goes **across** a place, they go from one side of it to the other.
*Hello Kitty walked **across** the road.*

act *verb*
acts, acting, acted

1 When you **act**, you do something.
*The police **acted** quickly to stop the fight.*

2 If you **act** in a play or film, you pretend to be one of the people in it.

active *adjective*

Someone who is **active** moves around a lot.
*Hello Kitty's grandmother is very **active** for her age.*

add *verb*
adds, adding, added

1 If you **add** one thing to another, you put it with the other thing.
Add the water to the flour.

2 If you **add** numbers together, you find out how many they make together.
Add three and six.

address *noun*
addresses

Your **address** is the name of the place where you live.

adjective *noun*
adjectives

An **adjective** is a word like "big" or "beautiful", that tells you more about a person or thing.

admire *verb*
admires, admiring, admired

If you **admire** something, you like it and think that it is very nice or very good.
Hello Kitty admired his painting.

adopt *verb*
adopts, adopting, adopted

If you **adopt** another person's child, you take them into your own family as your son or daughter.

adult *noun*
adults

An **adult** is a person who is not a child anymore.

adventure *noun*
adventures

An **adventure** is something exciting which you do, or which happens to you.
Hello Kitty had an adventure in the jungle.

adverb *noun*
adverbs

An **adverb** is a word like "slowly", "now", or "very", that tells you about how something is done.

aeroplane *noun*
aeroplanes

An **aeroplane** is a large vehicle with wings and engines that flies through the air.

afraid *adjective*

If you are **afraid**, you are frightened because you think that something bad will happen to you.
Hello Kitty is not afraid of the dark.

after

1   If something happens **after** another thing, it happens later than it.
    Hello Kitty watched television after dinner.

2   If you go **after** a person or thing, you follow them or chase them.
    Hello Kitty ran after her.

afternoon *noun*
afternoons

The **afternoon** is the part of each day between twelve noon and about six o'clock.

HELLO KITTY
SAFARI TOURS

again - allow

again

If something happens **again**, it happens another time.
Hello Kitty went to the park again yesterday.

against

1   If something is **against** another thing, it is touching it.
Hello Kitty leaned against the wall.

2   If you play **against** someone in a game, you try to beat them.
The two teams played against one another.

age *noun*
ages

Your **age** is the number of years that you have lived.

ago

You use **ago** to talk about a time in the past.
Hello Kitty's birthday was a week ago.

agree *verb*
agrees, agreeing, agreed

If you **agree** with someone, you think the same as they do about something.
I agree with you about him.

ahead

Someone who is **ahead** of another person is in front of them.
Hello Kitty ran ahead of us.

air *noun*

Air is the mixture of gases all around us that we breathe.
Hello Kitty opened the window and let in some air.

aircraft *noun*
aircraft

An **aircraft** is any vehicle which can fly.

airport *noun*
airports

An **airport** is a place where aeroplanes fly from and land.

alarm *noun*
alarms

An **alarm** is a piece of equipment that warns you of danger by making a noise.
The car alarm woke Hello Kitty up.

alien *noun*
aliens

In stories and films, an **alien** is a creature from another planet.

alike *adjective*

If people or things are **alike**, they are the same in some way.
The two girls looked alike.

alive *adjective*

If a person, an animal or a plant is **alive**, they are living and not dead.

all

You use **all** to talk about everything, everyone, or the whole of something.
The greedy boy ate all the cakes.

alligator *noun*
alligators

An **alligator** is a large reptile with a long body, a long mouth and sharp teeth. **Alligators'** mouths are in the shape of a letter U.

allow *verb*
allows, allowing, allowed

If you **allow** someone to do something, you let them do it.
Mum allowed Hello Kitty to go out and play.

a
b
c
d
e
f
g
h
i
j
k
l
m
n
o
p
q
r
s
t
u
v
w
x
y
z

3

A ❀

A B C D E F G H I J K L M N O P Q R S T U V W X Y Z

all right or alright *adjective*

If you say that something is **all right**, you mean that it is good enough.
Hello Kitty thought the film was all right.

almost

Almost means very nearly.
Hello Kitty almost missed the bus.

alone *adjective*

When you are **alone**, you are not with any other people.
Hello Kitty was alone in the room.

along

1   If you walk **along** a road or other place, you move towards one end of it.
Hello Kitty walked along the street.

2   If you bring something **along** when you go somewhere, you bring it with you.
Hello Kitty brought a present along to the party.

aloud

When you read or talk **aloud**, you read or talk so that other people can hear you.
She read the story aloud to Hello Kitty.

alphabet *noun*
alphabets

An **alphabet** is a set of letters that is used for writing words. The letters are arranged in a special order.
A is the first letter of the alphabet.

already

You use **already** to show that something has happened before the present time.
Hello Kitty is already here.

also

You use **also** to give more information about something.
I'm cold, and I'm also hungry.

always

If you **always** do something, you do it every time or all the time.
Hello Kitty is always early for school.

am

❤ Look at **be**
I am six years old.

amazing *adjective*

You say that something is **amazing** when it is a surprise and you like it.
Hello Kitty had an amazing holiday.

ambulance *noun*
ambulances

An **ambulance** is a vehicle for taking people to hospital.

amount *noun*
amounts

An **amount** of something is how much there is of it.
We only have a small amount of food.

amphibian *noun*
amphibians

An **amphibian** is an animal that lives both on land and in water, for example a frog or a toad.

❀ ancient - anything ❀

ancient *adjective*

Ancient means very old, or from a long time ago.
*They lived in an **ancient** castle.*

angry *adjective*
angrier, angriest

When you are **angry**, you feel very upset about something.
*She was **angry** at her brother for breaking the window.*

animal *noun*
animals

An **animal** is any creature that is alive, but not a plant or a person.

ankle *noun*
ankles

Your **ankle** is the part of your body where your foot joins your leg.
*I fell and twisted my **ankle**.*

annoy *verb*
annoys, annoying, annoyed

If something **annoys** you, it makes you angry and upset.
*It **annoys** Hello Kitty when people are rude.*

another

You use **another** to mean one more.
*Hello Kitty would like **another** cake.*

answer *verb*
answers, answering, answered

If you **answer** someone, you say something back to them.
*When I said hello, he didn't **answer**.*

ant *noun*
ants

Ants are small insects that live in large groups.

antelope *noun*
antelopes

An **antelope** is an animal that looks like a deer.

any

1   You use **any** to mean some of a thing.
    *Is there **any** juice left?*

2   You also use **any** to show that it does not matter which one.
    *Take **any** book you want.*

anybody

You use **anybody** to talk about a person, when it does not matter which one.
*Is there **anybody** there?*

anyone

You use **anyone** to talk about a person, when it does not matter who.
*Don't tell **anyone**.*

anything

You use **anything** to talk about a thing, when it does not matter which one.
*I can't see **anything**.*

a
b
c
d
e
f
g
h
i
j
k
l
m
n
o
p
q
r
s
t
u
v
w
x
y
z

5

A B C D E F G H I J K L M N O P Q R S T U V W X Y Z

anywhere

You use **anywhere** to talk about a place, when it does not matter which one.
You can go anywhere you like.

apart

1 When things are **apart**, there is a space or a distance between them.
The desks are too far apart.

2 If you take something **apart**, you take it to pieces.
He took his bike apart.

ape *noun*
apes

An **ape** is an animal like a large monkey with long, strong arms and no tail.

apologize *or* apologise *verb*
apologizes, apologizing, apologized

When you **apologize**, you say that you are sorry for something you have said or done.
He apologized for breaking the window.

appear *verb*
appears, appearing, appeared

When something **appears**, it becomes possible to see it
The sun appeared from behind the clouds.

apple *noun*
apples

An **apple** is a firm, round fruit with green, red, or yellow skin.

April *noun*

April is the month after March and before May. It has 30 days.
His birthday is in April.

apron *noun*
aprons

An **apron** is a large piece of cloth that you wear over your other clothes to keep them clean when you are cooking or painting.

are

Look at **be**
They are both in Hello Kitty's class.

area *noun*
areas

An **area** is a part of a place.
Hello Kitty lives in an area near the park.

aren't

Aren't is short for **are not**.
Hello Kitty's friends aren't here today.

argue *verb*
argues, arguing, argued

If you **argue** with someone, you talk about something that you do not agree about.
We argued about where to go.

argument *noun*
arguments

If you have an **argument** with someone, you talk about something that you do not agree about.
She had an argument with another girl.

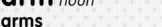
arm *noun*
arms

Your **arms** are the two parts of your body between your shoulders and your hands.
Hello Kitty stretched her arms out.

armchair *noun*
armchairs

An **armchair** is a big comfortable chair with parts on the sides for you to put your arms on.

army *noun*
armies

An **army** is a large group of soldiers who fight in a war.

around

1 **Around** means in a circle.
   There were lots of people around Hello Kitty.

2 You also use **around** to say that something is in every part of a place.
   Hello Kitty's toys lay around the room.

3 **Around** also means near to something.
   Hello Kitty left around noon.

arrange *verb*
arranges, arranging, arranged

1 If you **arrange** something, you make plans for it to happen.
   Hello Kitty arranged a party for her birthday.

2 If you **arrange** things somewhere, you put them in a way that looks tidy or pretty.
   Hello Kitty arranged the books in piles.

arrive *verb*
arrives, arriving, arrived

When you **arrive** at a place, you get there.
Hello Kitty arrived ten minutes early.

arrow *noun*
arrows

1 An **arrow** is a long, thin stick with a sharp point at one end.
   The soldiers used bows and arrows.

2 An **arrow** is also a sign that shows you which way to go.
   Follow the arrows along the path.

art *noun*

Art is something that someone has made for people to look at, for example a painting or drawing.

ask *verb*
asks, asking, asked

1 If you **ask** someone a question, you say that you want to know something.
   She asked the new pupil what his name was.

2 If you **ask** for something, you say that you want it.
   The boy asked for some more sweets.

asleep *adjective*

If you are **asleep**, you are sleeping.
The cat was asleep under the tree.

assembly *noun*
assemblies

An **assembly** is a group of people who meet together.
Hello Kitty was given a prize at school assembly.

assistant *noun*
assistants

An **assistant** is someone who helps another person in their work.

astronaut *noun*
astronauts

An **astronaut** is a person who travels in space.

A

A B C D E F G H I J K L M N O P Q R S T U V W X Y Z

ate
♥ Look at **eat**
My sister ate three biscuits at lunchtime.

atlas *noun*
atlases

An **atlas** is a book of maps.

attack *verb*
attacks, attacking, attacked

If someone **attacks** another person, they try to hurt them.

attention *noun*

If you pay **attention**, you watch and listen.
Hello Kitty always pays attention in class.

attract *verb*
attracts, attracting, attracted

If something **attracts** things to it, it makes them move towards it.
Magnets attract anything made of iron.

audience *noun*
audiences

An **audience** is all of the people who watch or listen to something, for example a film or a play.

August *noun*

August is the month after July and before September. It has 31 days.
Hello Kitty went on holiday in August.

aunt *noun*
aunts

Your **aunt** is the sister of your mother or father, or the wife of your uncle.

author *noun*
authors

An **author** is a person who writes books.

autumn *noun*
autumns

Autumn is the season after summer and before winter. In the **autumn** the weather usually becomes cooler and the leaves fall off the trees.

awake *adjective*

Someone who is **awake** is not sleeping.
Hello Kitty stayed awake until ten.

away

1 If someone moves **away** from a place, they move so that they are not there any more.
Hello Kitty walked away from the house.

2 If you put something **away**, you put it where it should be.
Put your books away before you go.

awful *adjective*

If something is **awful**, it is very bad.
There was an awful smell.

axe *noun*
axes

An **axe** is a tool with a handle and a big, sharp blade. It is used to chop wood.

Bb

baby *noun*
babies

A **baby** is a very young child.

back *noun*
backs

1   Your **back** is the part of your body from your neck to your bottom.
Hello Kitty was lying on her back in the grass.

2   The **back** of something is the side or part of it that is farthest from the front.
Hello Kitty was in a room at the back of the house.

backwards

1   If you move **backwards**, you move in the direction behind you.
Hello Kitty walked backwards.

2   If you do something **backwards**, you do it the opposite of the usual way.
Hello Kitty had her jumper on backwards.

bad *adjective*
worse, worst

1   Something that is **bad** is not nice or good.
The weather is bad today.

2   Someone who is **bad** does things they should not do.
Some bad boys stole the money.

badge *noun*
badges

A **badge** is a small piece of metal or plastic with words or a picture on it that you wear on your clothes.

badger *noun*
badgers

A **badger** is an animal that has a white head with two black stripes on it. **Badgers** live beneath the ground and come out at night.

bag
bags *noun*

A **bag** is a container that you use to hold or carry things.
Hello Kitty put her shoes in her bag.

bake *verb*
bakes, baking, baked

When you **bake** food, you cook it in an oven.

baker *noun*
bakers

A **baker** is a person who makes and sells bread and cakes.

balance *verb*
balances, balancing, balanced

When you **balance** something, you keep it steady and do not let it fall.
Hello Kitty balanced a book on her head.

ball *noun*
balls

A **ball** is a round thing that you kick, throw or catch in games.

ballet *noun*

Ballet is a kind of dance with special steps that often tells a story.

A B C D E F G H I J K L M N O P Q R S T U V W X Y Z

balloon *noun*
balloons
A **balloon** is a small bag made of thin rubber that you blow into to make it bigger.

banana *noun*
bananas
A **banana** is a long curved fruit with a thick yellow skin.

band *noun*
bands
1 A **band** is a group of people who play music together.
He plays the guitar in a band.

2 A **band** is also a narrow strip of material that you put around something.
Hello Kitty wore a band round her hair.

bandage *noun*
bandages
A **bandage** is a long strip of cloth that you wrap around a part of your body when you have hurt it.

bang *noun*
bangs
A **bang** is a sudden, loud noise.
The balloon burst with a bang.

bank *noun*
banks
1 A **bank** is a place where people can keep their money.
He got some money from the bank.

2 A **bank** is also the ground beside a river.
Hello Kitty walked along the bank.

bar *noun*
bars
A **bar** is a long, thin piece of wood or metal.
There were bars on the windows.

bare *adjective*
barer, barest
1 If a part of your body is **bare**, it is not covered by any clothes.
Hello Kitty's feet were bare.

2 If something is **bare**, it has nothing on top of it or inside it.
The cupboard was bare.

bark *verb*
barks, barking, barked
When a dog **barks**, it makes a short, loud noise.

barn *noun*
barns
A **barn** is a big building on a farm where animals and crops are kept.

base *noun*
bases
The **base** of something is the lowest part of it, or the part that it stands on.
Hello Kitty stood at the base of the stairs.

basket *noun*
baskets
A **basket** is a container that you use to hold or carry things. It is made from thin strips of material.

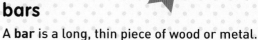

bat *noun*
bats

1　A **bat** is a special stick that you use to hit a ball in some games.
2　A **bat** is also a small animal that looks like a mouse with wings. **Bats** come out to fly at night.

bath *noun*
baths

A **bath** is a long container that you fill with water and sit in to wash yourself.

bathroom *noun*
bathrooms

A **bathroom** is a room with a bath or shower in it.

battery *noun*
batteries

A **battery** is a small tube or box for storing electricity. You put **batteries** in things like toys and radios to make them work.
*Hello Kitty's clock needs a new **battery**.*

be *verb*
am, is, are, being, was, were, been

1　You use **be** to say what a person or thing is like.
*She **is** very young.*
2　You also use **be** to say that something is there.
*There **is** an apple tree in Hello Kitty's garden.*

beach *noun*
beaches

A **beach** is the land by the edge of the sea. It is covered with sand or stones.

bead *noun*
beads

A **bead** is a small piece of glass, wood or plastic with a hole through the middle. You put **beads** on a string to make necklaces or bracelets.

beak *noun*
beaks

A bird's **beak** is the hard part of its mouth.

bean *noun*
beans

A **bean** is the small seed of some plants that you can eat as a vegetable.

bear *noun*
bears

A **bear** is a big, strong animal with thick fur and sharp claws.

beard *noun*
beards

A **beard** is the hair that grows on a man's chin and cheeks.

beat *verb*
beats, beating, beat, beaten

1　If you **beat** something, you keep hitting it.
*Hello Kitty **beat** the drum with a stick.*
2　If you **beat** someone in a game or a competition, you do better than they do.
*Hello Kitty **beat** everyone in the race.*

beautiful *adjective*

If something is **beautiful**, it is very nice to look at or to listen to.
*Hello Kitty painted a **beautiful** picture.*

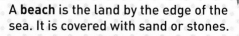

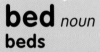

B

became
♥ Look at **become**
She became very angry.

because
You use **because** to say why something happens.
Hello Kitty went to bed because she was tired.

become verb
becomes, becoming, became, become

If one thing **becomes** another thing, it starts to be that thing.
The weather became cold.

bed noun
beds

A **bed** is a piece of furniture that you lie on when you sleep.

bedroom noun
bedrooms

A **bedroom** is a room with a bed in it where you sleep.

bedtime noun
bedtimes

Your **bedtime** is the time when you usually go to bed.
Hello Kitty's bedtime is at eight o'clock.

bee noun
bees

A **bee** is an insect with wings and black and yellow stripes on its body. **Bees** live in large groups and make honey.

been
♥ Look at **be**
We have always been good friends.

beetle noun
beetles

A **beetle** is an insect with hard wings that cover its body when it is not flying.

before
If one thing happens **before** another thing, it happens earlier than it.
Hello Kitty's birthday is just before his.

began
♥ Look at **begin**
Hello Kitty began to dance.

begin verb
begins, beginning, began, begun

If you **begin** to do something, you start to do it.
You can begin to write now.

begun
♥ Look at **begin**
Hello Kitty has begun to play the piano.

behave *verb*
behaves, behaving, behaved

1 The way you **behave** is the way that you do and say things.
She behaves like a baby.

2 If you **behave** yourself, you are good.
You can come if you behave yourself.

behind

If something is **behind** another thing, it is at the back of it.
Hello Kitty stood behind the desk.

believe *verb*
believes, believing, believed

If you **believe** something, you think that it is true.
Hello Kitty believes in fairies.

bell *noun*
bells

A **bell** is a piece of metal in the shape of a cup that rings when you shake it or hit it.

belong *verb*
belongs, belonging, belonged

1 If something **belongs** to you, it is yours.
The book belongs to her.

2 If you **belong** to a group of people, you are one of them.
He belongs to our team.

3 If something **belongs** somewhere, that is where it should be.
Your toys belong in your room.

below

If something is **below** another thing, it is lower down than it.
Hello Kitty's slippers are below her bed.

belt *noun*
belts

A **belt** is a band of leather or cloth that you wear around your waist.

bench *noun*
benches

A **bench** is a long seat that two or more people can sit on.

bend *verb*
bends, bending, bent

When you **bend** something, you change its shape so that it is not straight any more.
Bend your legs when you do this exercise.

beneath

If something is **beneath** another thing, it is below it.
Hello Kitty's bag was beneath the table.

bent

♥ Look at **bend**
Hello Kitty bent to pick up the bags.

berry *noun*
berries

A **berry** is a small, soft fruit that grows on a bush or a tree.

beside

If something is **beside** another thing, it is next to it.
Hello Kitty sat down beside me.

best

If you say that something is **best**, you mean that it is better than all the others.
Hello Kitty is my best friend.

a
b
c
d
e
f
g
h
i
j
k
l
m
n
o
p
q
r
s
t
u
v
w
x
y
z

A
B ❀
C
D
E
F
G
H
I
J
K
L
M
N
O
P
Q
R
S
T
U
V
W
X
Y
Z

better

1   You use **better** to mean that a thing is very good compared to another thing.
Hello Kitty's painting is better than mine.

2   If you feel **better**, you do not feel ill any more.
Hello Kitty feels much better today.

between

If you are **between** two things, one of them is on one side of you and the other is on the other side.
Hello Kitty stood between her two friends.

bicycle *noun*
bicycles

A **bicycle** is a vehicle with two wheels. You push the pedals with your feet to make the wheels turn.

big *adjective*
bigger, biggest

A person or thing that is **big** is large in size.
Hello Kitty's friend lives in a big house.

bike *noun*
bikes

A **bike** is a bicycle or motorbike.

bin *noun*
bins

A **bin** is a container that you put rubbish in.

bird *noun*
birds

A **bird** is an animal with feathers wings, and a beak. Most **birds** can fly.

birthday *noun*
birthdays

Your **birthday** is the date that you were born.
Hello Kitty gave me a present on my birthday.

biscuit *noun*
biscuits

A **biscuit** is a kind of small, hard, dry cake.

bit *noun*
bits

A **bit** of something is a small amount of it, or a small part of it.
Can I have a bit of bread please?

bite *verb*
bites, biting, bit, bitten

If you **bite** something, you use your teeth to cut into it.
The dog tried to bite him.

black *noun*

Black is the colour of the sky at night.
The car is black.

blackboard *noun*
blackboards

A **blackboard** is a flat, black surface that you write on with chalk in a classroom.

14

blade noun
blades

A **blade** is the flat, sharp part of a knife that you use to cut things.

blame verb
blames, blaming, blamed

If you **blame** someone for something bad, you think that they made it happen.
Mum blamed me for making the mess.

blanket noun
blankets

A **blanket** is a large, thick piece of cloth that you put on a bed to keep you warm.

blew

♥ Look at **blow**
He blew on his hands to keep them warm.

blind adjective

Someone who is **blind** cannot see.

block noun
blocks

A **block** of something is a large piece of it with straight sides.
Hello Kitty made a house with blocks of wood.

blood noun

Blood is the red liquid that moves around inside your body.

blouse noun
blouses

A **blouse** is something a girl or woman can wear. It covers the top part of the body and has buttons down the front.

blow verb
blows, blowing, blew, blown

1 When the wind **blows**, it moves the air.
The wind blew in our faces.

2 When you **blow**, you push air out of your mouth.
The wind blew the leaves down the path.

blue noun

Blue is the colour of the sky on a sunny day.
Hello Kitty's new dress is blue.

blunt adjective
blunter, bluntest

Something that is **blunt** does not have a sharp point or edge.
Hello Kitty's pencil is blunt.

boat noun
boats

A **boat** is a small vehicle that carries people on water.

body noun
bodies

A person's or animal's **body** is all their parts.
It's fun to stretch and twist your body.

boil verb
boils, boiling, boiled

1 When water **boils**, it becomes very hot, and you can see bubbles in it and steam coming from it.

2 When you **boil** food, you cook it in water that is boiling.

bone noun
bones

Your **bones** are the hard parts inside your body.
I broke a bone in my leg.

a
b
c
d
e
f
g
h
i
j
k
l
m
n
o
p
q
r
s
t
u
v
w
x
y
z

A | B | C | D | E | F | G | H | I | J | K | L | M | N | O | P | Q | R | S | T | U | V | W | X | Y | Z

bonfire *noun*
bonfires

A **bonfire** is a big fire that is made outside.

book *noun*
books

A **book** is a set of pages with words or pictures on them, that are held together inside a cover.

boot *noun*
boots

A **boot** is a kind of shoe that covers your foot and the lower part of your leg.

bored *adjective*

If you are **bored**, you feel annoyed because you have nothing to do.

boring *adjective*

If something is **boring**, it is not interesting.

born *verb*

When a baby is **born**, it comes out of its mother's body.
*My sister was **born** three years ago.*

borrow *verb*
borrows, borrowing, borrowed

If you **borrow** something from someone, they let you have it for a short time and then you give it back.
*Can I **borrow** your pen, please?*

both

You use **both** to mean two people or two things together.
*Hello Kitty put **both** books in the drawer.*

bottle *noun*
bottles

A **bottle** is a container made of glass or plastic that holds liquid.

bottom *noun*
bottoms

1 The **bottom** of something is its lowest part.
2 Your **bottom** is the part of your body that you sit on.

bought

♥ Look at **buy**
*Hello Kitty **bought** a pink balloon.*

bounce *verb*
bounces, bouncing, bounced

When something **bounces**, it hits another thing and then moves away from it again.
*Hello Kitty's ball **bounced** across the floor.*

bow *verb*
bows, bowing, bowed

When you **bow**, you bend your body towards someone as a polite way of saying hello or thanking them.
*They all **bowed** to the king.*

bow noun
bows

1 A **bow** is a knot with two loose ends that you use to tie laces and ribbons.

2 A **bow** is also a long, curved piece of wood with a string stretched between the two ends, that is used to send arrows through the air.

bowl noun
bowls

A **bowl** is a round container that you use to hold food or drink.

box noun
boxes

A **box** is a container with a hard, straight bottom and sides, and usually a lid.

boy noun
boys

A **boy** is a male child.

bracelet noun
bracelets

A **bracelet** is a chain or a band that you wear around your wrist.

brain noun
brains

Your **brain** is inside your head. It controls your body and lets you think and feel things.

branch noun
branches

The **branches** of a tree are the parts that grow out from its trunk and have leaves on them.

brave adjective
braver, bravest

If you are **brave**, you are not afraid of something dangerous.

bread noun

Bread is a food that is made from flour and water and baked in an oven.

break verb
breaks, breaking, broke, broken

1 When something **breaks**, it goes into pieces. *Hello Kitty dropped a plate and it broke.*

2 When a machine **breaks**, it stops working. *The television broke last night.*

breakfast noun
breakfasts

Breakfast is the first meal of the day.

breathe verb
breathes, breathing, breathed

When you **breathe**, air goes in and out of your body through your nose or your mouth.

brick noun
bricks

Bricks are small blocks of baked earth used for building.

a
c
d
e
f
g
h
i
j
k
l
m
n
o
p
q
r
s
t
u
v
w
x
y
z

A
B ❀
C
D
E
F
G
H
I
J
K
L
M
N
O
P
Q
R
S
T
U
V
W
X
Y
Z

bride *noun*
brides

A **bride** is a woman who is getting married.

bridegroom *noun*
bridegrooms

A **bridegroom** is a man who is getting married.

bridge *noun*
bridges

A **bridge** is something that is built over a river, a road, or a railway so that people can get across it.

bright *adjective*
brighter, brightest

1   A **bright** colour is very easy to see.
    *Hello Kitty wore a **bright** red dress.*

2   Something that is **bright** shines with a lot of light.
    *The sun is very **bright** today.*

brilliant *adjective*

Something that is **brilliant** is very good.
*Hello Kitty thought the film was **brilliant**.*

bring *verb*
brings, bringing, brought

If you **bring** something, you take it with you when you go somewhere.
*Hello Kitty wants to **bring** a friend to the party.*

broke

♥ Look at **break**
*I'm sorry I **broke** the radio.*

broken *adjective*

If something is **broken**, it is in pieces.
*All of his toys are **broken**.*

broom *noun*
brooms

A **broom** is a brush with a long handle that you use to sweep the floor.

brother *noun*
brothers

Your **brother** is a boy or a man who has the same mother and father as you do.

brought

♥ Look at **bring**
*Hello Kitty **brought** some food for the picnic.*

brown *noun*

Brown is the colour of earth or wood.
*Her eyes are dark **brown**.*

🌸 br uise - bu rn 🌸

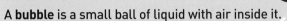

bruise *noun*
bruises

A **bruise** is a purple mark on your skin that appears if something hits a part of your body.
*She has a big **bruise** on her leg.*

bubble *noun*
bubbles

A **bubble** is a small ball of liquid with air inside it.

bucket *noun*
buckets

A **bucket** is a deep, round container with a handle that you use to hold or carry liquids.

buckle *noun*
buckles

A **buckle** is something you use to fasten a belt, a shoe or a bag.

bud *noun*
buds

A **bud** is a small, new part on a tree or plant that grows into a leaf or a flower.

build *verb*
builds, building, built

If you **build** something, you make it by putting the parts of it together.
*They are going to **build** the school here.*

building *noun*
buildings

A **building** is a place with walls and a roof.
*Houses, shops and schools are all **buildings**.*

built

💜 Look at **build**
*We **built** our house on a hill.*

bulb *noun*
bulbs

A **bulb** is the part of a lamp that is made of glass and gives out light.

bull *noun*
bulls

A **bull** is a male cow.
Bulls have horns.

bump *verb*
bumps, bumping, bumped

If you **bump** something, or **bump** into it, you hit it without meaning to.
*Hello Kitty **bumped** the table with her bag.*

bunch *noun*
bunches

A **bunch** of things is a group of them.
*Hello Kitty found a **bunch** of keys.*

bundle *noun*
bundles

A **bundle** is a lot of clothes, sticks or other things that are fastened together.

buried

💜 Look at **bury**
*The pirates **buried** the gold beneath a tree.*

burn *verb*
burns, burning, burned or **burnt**

1 If you **burn** something, you destroy it or damage it with fire.
*He **burned** all the rubbish.*

2 If you **burn** yourself, you touch something that is hot and get hurt.
*I **burned** myself on the hot iron.*

3 If something is **burning**, it is on fire.
*The bonfire is still **burning**.*

a
🌸 b
c
d
e
f
g
h
i
j
k
l
m
n
o
p
q
r
s
t
u
v
w
x
y
z

19

burst *verb*
bursts, bursting, burst

When something **bursts**, it breaks open suddenly.
*Hello Kitty's bag **burst** and everything fell out of it.*

bury *verb*
buries, burying, buried

If you **bury** something, you put it into a hole in the ground and cover it up.
*Squirrels **bury** nuts to eat in the winter.*

bus *noun*
buses

A **bus** is a large vehicle that carries lots of people.
*Hello Kitty goes to school on the **bus**.*

bush *noun*
bushes

A **bush** is a plant with lots of leaves and branches that is smaller than a tree.

busy *adjective*
busier, busiest

1 If you are **busy**, you have a lot of things to do.
*Hello Kitty was **busy** helping her mother.*

2 A **busy** place is full of people.
*The shops are **busy** today.*

butcher *noun*
butchers

A **butcher** is a person who sells meat.

butter *noun*

Butter is a soft yellow food that is made from cream. You spread it on bread or cook with it.

butterfly *noun*
butterflies

A **butterfly** is an insect with four large wings.

button *noun*
buttons

Buttons are small, round things on clothes that you push through holes to fasten the clothes together.

buy *verb*
buys, buying, bought

If you **buy** something, you pay money so that you can have it.
*Hello Kitty went into the shop to **buy** sweets.*

buzz *verb*
buzzes, buzzing, buzzed

If something **buzzes**, it makes a sound like a bee makes when it flies.
*An insect **buzzed** around Hello Kitty's head.*

Cc

a
b
c
d
e
f
g
h
i
j
k
l
m
n
o
p
q
r
s
t
u
v
w
x
y
z

cabbage *noun*
cabbages

A **cabbage** is a round vegetable with green, white, or purple leaves.

cage *noun*
cages

A **cage** is a box or a room made of bars where you keep birds or animals.

cake *noun*
cakes

A **cake** is a sweet food made from flour, eggs, sugar, and butter that you bake in an oven.

calculator *noun*
calculators

A **calculator** is a small machine that you use to do sums.

calendar *noun*
calendars

A **calendar** is a list of all the days, weeks, and months in a year.

calf *noun*
calves

1   A **calf** is a young cow.

2   Your **calves** are also the thick parts at the backs of your legs, between your ankles and your knees.

call *verb*
calls, calling, called

1   If you **call** someone something, you give them a name.
    I called my cat Pippin.

2   If you **call** something, you say it in a loud voice.
    Someone called Hello Kitty's name.

3   If you **call** someone, you talk to them on the telephone.
    I'll call you tomorrow.

calves

♥ Look at **calf**
My calves hurt.

came

♥ Look at **come**
Hello Kitty's friends came to play at her house.

camel *noun*
camels

A **camel** is a large animal with one or two big lumps on its back. **Camels** live in hot, dry places and carry people and things.

camera *noun*
cameras

A **camera** is a machine that you use to take pictures.

camp *noun*
camps

A **camp** is a place where people live in tents for a short time.

A B C D E F G H I J K L M N O P Q R S T U V W X Y Z

can *verb*
could

If you **can** do something, you are able to do it.
*Hello Kitty **can** swim.*

can *noun*
cans

A **can** is a metal container for food or drink.
*She opened a **can** of soup.*

candle *noun*
candles

A **candle** is a stick of wax with a piece of string through the middle that you burn to give you light.

cannot *verb*

If you **cannot** do something, you are not able to do it.
*Hello Kitty **cannot** find her book.*

can't

Can't is short for **cannot**.
*Hello Kitty **can't** come out to play.*

capital *noun*
capitals

1 The **capital** of a country is the main city, where the country's leaders work.
*Paris is the **capital** of France.*

2 A **capital** is also a big letter of the alphabet, for example A or R.

car *noun*
cars

A **car** is a vehicle with four wheels and an engine that can carry a small number of people.

card *noun*
cards

1 **Card** is stiff paper.

2 A **card** is a folded piece of stiff paper that has a picture on the front and a message inside. You send **cards** to people at special times, like birthdays.

3 **Cards** are pieces of stiff paper with numbers or pictures on them that you use for playing games.

cardboard *noun*

Cardboard is very thick, stiff paper that is used for making boxes.

care *verb*
cares, caring, cared

1 If you **care** about something, you think that it is important.
*He doesn't **care** about the way he looks.*

2 If you **care** for a person or an animal, you look after them.
*Hello Kitty **cares** for her pet.*

careful *adjective*

If you are **careful**, you think about what you are doing so that you do not make any mistakes.
*Be **careful** when you cross the road.*

careless *adjective*

If you are **careless**, you do not think about what you are doing, so that you make mistakes.
*It was **careless** of me to forget my keys.*

carpet *noun*
carpets

A **carpet** is a thick, soft cover for a floor.

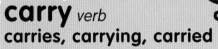

carrot *noun*
carrots

A **carrot** is a long, orange vegetable.

carry *verb*
carries, carrying, carried

If you **carry** something, you hold it and take it somewhere with you.
Hello Kitty is carrying an icecream.

carton *noun*
cartons

A **carton** is a container made of plastic or cardboard that is used to hold food or drink.
Hello Kitty lifted a carton of milk.

cartoon *noun*
cartoons

1 A **cartoon** is a funny drawing.
2 A **cartoon** is also a film that uses drawings, not real people or things.

case *noun*
cases

A **case** is a container that is used to hold or carry something.
Hello Kitty put the camera in its case.

castle *noun*
castles

A **castle** is a large building with very thick, high walls. Most **castles** were built a long time ago to keep the people inside safe from their enemies.

cat *noun*
cats

A **cat** is an animal that is covered with fur and has a long tail. People often keep small **cats** as pets. Large **cats**, for example lions and tigers, are wild.

catch *verb*
catches, catching, caught

1 If you **catch** something that is moving, you take hold of it while it is in the air.
Hello Kitty tried to catch the ball.
2 If you **catch** a bus or a train, you get on it.
Hello Kitty caught the bus to school.
3 If you **catch** an illness, you become ill with it.
He caught measles.

caterpillar *noun*
caterpillars

A **caterpillar** is a small animal that looks like a worm with lots of short legs. **Caterpillars** turn into butterflies or moths.

cattle *noun*

Cattle are cows and bulls.
There were cattle in the field.

caught

♥ Look at **catch**
Hello Kitty jumped and caught the ball.

cauliflower *noun*
cauliflowers

A **cauliflower** is a big, round, white vegetable with green leaves.

cave *noun*
caves

A **cave** is a big hole in the side of a hill or a mountain, or beneath the ground.

CD *noun*
CDs

CD is short for compact disc.
This is Hello Kitty's favourite CD.

a
b
❀ c
d
e
f
g
h
i
j
k
l
m
n
o
p
q
r
s
t
u
v
w
x
y
z

ceiling *noun*
ceilings

A **ceiling** is the part of a room that is above your head.

centimetre *noun*
centimetres

A **centimetre** is used for measuring the length of something. There are ten millimetres in a **centimetre**, and one hundred **centimetres** in a metre.

centre *noun*
centres

The **centre** of something is the middle of it.
Hello Kitty stood in the centre of the room.

cereal *noun*
cereals

1   A **cereal** is a food made from grains that you eat with milk for breakfast.

2   A **cereal** is also a kind of plant, for example wheat or rice. The seeds of **cereals** are used for food.

chain *noun*
chains

A **chain** is a row of rings made of metal that are joined together in a line.

chair *noun*
chairs

A **chair** is a seat with a back and four legs, for one person.
Hello Kitty got up from her chair.

chalk *noun*

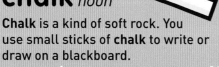

Chalk is a kind of soft rock. You use small sticks of **chalk** to write or draw on a blackboard.

change *verb*
changes, changing, changed

1   When you **change** something, or when it **changes**, it becomes different.
The caterpillar changed into a butterfly.

2   When you **change**, you put on different clothes.
Hello Kitty changed to go to the party.

change *noun*

Change is the money that you get back when you pay too much for something.

chapter *noun*
chapters

A **chapter** is a part of a book.
Hello Kitty's book has ten chapters.

character *noun*
characters

1   Your **character** is the kind of person you are.

2   A **character** is also a person in a story or a film.

A B C D E F G H I J K L M N O P Q R S T U V W X Y Z

charge *verb*
charges, charging, charged
If someone **charges** you an amount of money for something, they ask you to pay that amount for it.
They charged us too much for our meal.

chase *verb*
chases, chasing, chased
If you **chase** someone, you run after them and try to catch them.
The dog chased the cat.

cheap *adjective*
cheaper, cheapest
If something is **cheap,** you do not have to pay a lot of money for it.
Milk is very cheap in this shop.

check *verb*
checks, checking, checked
If you **check** something, you make sure that it is right.
The teacher checked Hello Kitty's homework.

cheek *noun*
cheeks
Your **cheeks** are the sides of your face below your eyes.
Thomas Bear's cheeks were red.

cheer *verb*
cheers, cheering, cheered
When people **cheer,** they shout to show that they like something.
We all cheered when Hello Kitty won the race.

cheerful *adjective*
Someone who is **cheerful** is happy.

cheese *noun*
Cheese is a solid food that is made from milk.

cheetah *noun*
cheetahs
A **cheetah** is a big wild cat with yellow fur and black spots.

cherry *noun*
cherries

A **cherry** is a small, round fruit with a hard stone in the middle. **Cherries** are red, black, or yellow.

chew *verb*
chews, chewing, chewed
When you **chew** food, you use your teeth to break it up in your mouth before you swallow it.

chick *noun*
chicks
A **chick** is a very young bird.

chicken *noun*
chickens
1   A **chicken** is a bird that is kept on a farm for its eggs and meat.
2   **Chicken** is the meat that comes from chickens.

child *noun*
children
A **child** is a young boy or girl.

chimney *noun*
chimneys
A **chimney** is a long pipe above a fire. Smoke from the fire goes up the **chimney** and out of the building.

chimpanzee *noun*
chimpanzees
A **chimpanzee** is a kind of small ape with dark fur.

chin *noun*
chins

Your **chin** is the part of your face below your mouth.
A black beard covered his chin.

chip *noun*
chips

Chips or potato **chips** are thin pieces of potato fried in hot oil.

chip *verb*
chips, chipping, chipped

If you **chip** something, you break a small piece off it by accident.
I chipped my tooth when I fell.

chocolate *noun*
chocolates

Chocolate is a sweet brown food that is used to make sweets, cakes, and drinks.

choose *verb*
chooses, choosing, chose, chosen

If you **choose** something, you decide to have it.
You can choose any book you want.

chop *verb*
chops, chopping, chopped

If you **chop** something, you cut it into pieces with a knife or an axe.
He chopped some wood for the fire.

chose

💜 Look at **choose**
Hello Kitty chose a dress to wear.

chosen

💜 Look at **choose**
Hello Kitty has chosen which film to watch.

circle *noun*
circles

A **circle** is a round shape.

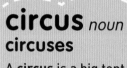

circus *noun*
circuses

A **circus** is a big tent where you go to see clowns and animals.

city *noun*
cities

A **city** is a very big town where a lot of people live and work.

clap *verb*
claps, clapping, clapped

When you **clap**, you hit your hands together to make a loud noise. People **clap** to show that they like something.
Everyone clapped at the end of the show.

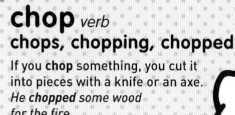

class *noun*
classes

A **class** is a group of people who are taught together.
He is in Hello Kitty's class at school.

classroom *noun*
classrooms

A **classroom** is a room in a school where children have lessons.

claw *noun*
claws

A bird's or an animal's **claws** are the hard, sharp, curved parts at the end of its feet.

clean *adjective*
cleaner, cleanest

Something that is **clean** does not have any dirt or marks on it.
Hello Kitty made sure her hands were clean.

clean *verb*
cleans, cleaning, cleaned

When you **clean** something, you take all the dirt off it.
Hello Kitty cleans her teeth before bedtime.

clear *adjective*
clearer, clearest

1 If something is **clear**, it is easy to understand, to see, or to hear.
He gave us clear instructions on what to do.

2 If something like glass or plastic is **clear**, you can see through it.
The liquid was in a clear plastic bottle.

3 If a place is **clear**, it does not have anything there that you do not want.
You can cross the road when it is clear.

clear *verb*
clears, clearing, cleared

When you **clear** a place, you take away all the things you do not want there.
Hello Kitty cleared the table.

clever *adjective*
cleverer, cleverest

Someone who is **clever** can learn and understand things quickly.
Hello Kitty is very clever at maths.

cliff *noun*
cliffs

A **cliff** is a hill with one side that is very steep. **Cliffs** are often beside the sea.

climb *verb*
climbs, climbing, climbed

If you **climb** something, you move towards the top of it. You sometimes use your hands as well as your feet when you **climb**.
Hello Kitty climbed the tree in the garden.

cloak *noun*
cloaks

A **cloak** is a very loose coat without sleeves.

clock *noun*
clocks

A **clock** is a machine that shows you the time.

close *verb*
closes, closing, closed

When you **close** something, you shut it.
Please close the door behind you.

close *adjective*
closer, closest

If something is **close** to another thing, it is near it.
Hello Kitty's house is close to the park.

A B C ❀ D E F G H I J K L M N O P Q R S T U V W X Y Z

cloth *noun*
cloths

1 **Cloth** is material that is used to make things like clothes and curtains.

2 A **cloth** is a piece of material that you use to clean something.

clothes *noun*

Clothes are the things that people wear, for example shirts, trousers, and dresses.

cloud *noun*
clouds

A **cloud** is a white or grey shape that you see in the sky. **Clouds** are made of tiny drops of water that sometimes turn into rain.

clown *noun*
clowns

A **clown** is a person who wears funny clothes and does silly things to make people laugh.

coat *noun*
coats

You wear a **coat** on top of your other clothes when you go outside.

cobweb *noun*
cobwebs

A **cobweb** is a very thin net that a spider makes to catch insects.

coconut *noun*
coconuts

A **coconut** is a very large nut that has a very hard shell and is white inside. **Coconuts** are full of a liquid called **coconut** milk.

coffee *noun*

Coffee is a drink. You make it by pouring hot water on **coffee** beans.
Coffee beans grow on a coffee plant.

coin *noun*
coins

A **coin** is a round, flat piece of metal that is used as money.

cold *adjective*
colder, coldest

1 If you are **cold**, you do not feel comfortable because you are not warm enough.
Wear a jumper if you are cold.

2 If something is **cold**, it is not hot.
The weather is very cold.

cold *noun*
colds

When you have a **cold**, you sneeze and cough a lot, and you have a sore throat.

collar *noun*
collars

1 The **collar** of a shirt or jacket is the part that goes around your neck.

2 A **collar** is also a band that goes around the neck of a dog or cat.

collect *verb*
collects, collecting, collected

1 If you **collect** things, you bring them together.
He collected wood for the fire.

2 If you **collect** someone from a place, you go there and take them away.
Mum collected Hello Kitty from school.

colour *noun*
colours

Red, blue and yellow are the main **colours**. You can mix them together to make other **colours**.

comb *noun*
combs

A **comb** is a flat piece of metal or plastic with very thin points that you use to make your hair tidy.

come *verb*
comes, coming, came, come

When you **come** to a place, you move towards it or arrive there.
Hello Kitty came into the room.

comfortable *adjective*

If something is **comfortable**, it makes you feel good.
Hello Kitty sat in a very comfortable chair.

comic *noun*
comics

A **comic** is a magazine with stories that are told in pictures.

common *adjective*

If things are **common**, you see lots of them around, or they happen often.
Foxes are quite common in this area.

compact disc *noun*
compact discs

A **compact disc** is a round, flat piece of plastic that has music or information on it. **Compact discs** are also called CDs.

competition *noun*
competitions

When you are in a **competition**, you try to show that you are the best at something.
Hello Kitty won the painting competition.

complete *adjective*

If something is **complete**, none of it is missing.
Hello Kitty has a complete set of crayons.

computer *noun*
computers

A **computer** is a machine that can store a lot of information and can work things out very quickly.
Hello Kitty played games on her computer.

confused *adjective*

If you are **confused**, you do not understand what is happening, or you do not know what to do.
She was confused about where to go.

consonant *noun*
consonants

A **consonant** is any letter of the alphabet that is not a, e, i, o, or u.
The word "book" has two consonants in it.

container *noun*
containers

A **container** is something that you use to keep things in, for example a box or a bottle.

control - count

control *verb*
controls, controlling, controlled

If you **control** something, you can make it do what you want.
*I can **control** the speed by pressing this button.*

cook *verb*
cooks, cooking, cooked

When you **cook** food, you make it hot and get it ready to eat.
*Hello Kitty's mother was **cooking** dinner.*

cooker *noun*
cookers

A **cooker** is a machine that you use to cook food.

cool *adjective*
cooler, coolest

Something that is **cool** is quite cold.
*Hello Kitty put the milk in the fridge to keep it **cool**.*

copy *noun*
copies

A **copy** is something that is made to look like another thing.
*Hello Kitty made a **copy** of the drawing.*

corn *noun*

Corn is a long vegetable. It is covered with yellow seeds that you eat.

corner *noun*
corners

A **corner** is a place where two sides join together.
*Hello Kitty reached the **corner** of the street.*

correct *adjective*

If something is **correct**, there are no mistakes.

cost *noun*
costs

The **cost** of something is the amount of money you need to buy it.
*The **cost** of the holiday was too high.*

cot *noun*
cots

A **cot** is a bed for a baby, with high sides to stop the baby from falling out.

cotton *noun*

1 **Cotton** is a kind of cloth that is made from the **cotton** plant.

2 **Cotton** is also thread that you use to sew

cough *verb*
coughs, coughing, coughed

When you **cough**, you make air come out of your throat with a sudden, loud noise.
*The smoke made us **cough**.*

could *verb*

If you say you **could** do something, you mean that you were able to do it. **Could** comes from the word **can**.
*Hello Kitty **could** see through the window.*

couldn't

Couldn't is short for **could not**.
*Hello Kitty **couldn't** open the door.*

count *verb*
counts, counting, counted

1 When you **count**, you say numbers in order, one after the other.
*The clever child **counted** from one to twenty.*

2 When you **count** all the things in a group, you add them up to see how many there are.
*The teacher **counted** the children in Hello Kitty's class.*

30

country noun
countries

1 A **country** is a part of the world with its own people and laws.
He lives in a different country.

2 The **country** is land that is away from towns and cities. There are farms and woods in the **country**.
Hello Kitty went for a walk in the country.

cousin noun
cousins

Your **cousin** is the son or daughter of your uncle or aunt.

cover verb
covers, covering, covered

If you **cover** something, you put another thing over it.
Hello Kitty covered the table with a cloth.

cover noun
covers

A **cover** is something that you put over another thing.
Put a cover over the sofa to keep it clean.

cow noun
cows

A **cow** is a large animal that is kept on farms because it gives milk.

crab noun
crabs

A **crab** is an animal with a hard shell that lives in the sea. **Crabs** have large claws on their front legs.

crack verb
cracks, cracking, cracked

If something **cracks**, it becomes damaged, and lines appear on the surface where it has broken.
The window cracked.

crane noun
cranes

1 A **crane** is a tall machine that can lift very heavy things.

2 A **crane** is also a large bird with a long neck and long legs. **Cranes** live near water.

crash noun
crashes

1 A **crash** is an accident when a vehicle hits something.
There was a car crash outside the school.

2 A **crash** is also a sudden, loud noise.
He dropped the plates with a crash.

crawl verb
crawls, crawling, crawled

When you **crawl**, you move along on your hands and knees.
The baby crawled along the floor.

crayon noun
crayons

Crayons are pencils or sticks of wax in different colours that you use for drawing.

cream noun

Cream is a thick liquid that is made from milk. You can use it in cooking or pour it over puddings.

a b **c** d e f g h i j k l m n o p q r s t u v w x y z

creature *noun*
creatures

A **creature** is anything that is alive, but is not a plant.
Many creatures live in the forest.

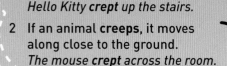

creep *verb*
creeps, creeping, crept

1 If you **creep** somewhere, you move in a very slow and quiet way.
Hello Kitty crept up the stairs.

2 If an animal **creeps**, it moves along close to the ground.
The mouse crept across the room.

crew *noun*
crews

A **crew** is a group of people who work together on a ship or an aeroplane.

cricket *noun*
crickets

1 **Cricket** is a game where two teams take turns to hit a ball with a bat and run up and down.

2 A **cricket** is also a small jumping insect that rubs its wings together to make a high sound.

crop *noun*
crops

Crops are plants that people grow for food, for example potatoes and wheat.

cross *verb*
crosses, crossing, crossed

If you **cross** something, you go from one side of it to the other.
Hello Kitty knows you must cross the road where it is safe.

cross *noun*
crosses

A **cross** is a mark that you write. It looks like **X** or **+**.
She put a cross beside Hello Kitty's name.

cross *adjective*
crosser, crossest

If you are **cross**, you feel angry about something.
Mum was cross because we were late.

crowd *noun*
crowds

A **crowd** is a lot of people together in one place.
A big crowd came to see the game.

crown *noun*
crowns

A **crown** is a circle made of gold or silver and jewels that kings and queens wear on their heads.

cry *verb*
cries, crying, cried

When you **cry**, tears come from your eyes. People **cry** when they are sad or hurt.
The baby started to cry.

A B C D E F G H I J K L M N O P Q R S T U V W X Y Z

cry *noun*
cries

A **cry** is a loud sound that you make with your voice.
Hello Kitty heard the cry of a bird.

cub *noun*
cubs

A **cub** is a young wild animal, for example a young bear or lion.

cube *noun*
cubes

A **cube** is a solid shape with six sides that are all squares.
A dice is in the shape of a cube.

cucumber *noun*
cucumbers

A **cucumber** is a long, thin, green vegetable that you eat in salads.

cuddle *verb*
cuddles, cuddling, cuddled

If you **cuddle** someone, you put your arms around them and hold them close to you.

cup *noun*
cups

A **cup** is a small, round container with a handle. You drink things like tea and coffee from a **cup**.

cupboard *noun*
cupboards

A **cupboard** is a piece of furniture with a door and shelves that you keep things in.
The cupboard was full of Hello Kitty's toys.

curl *noun*
curls

A **curl** is a piece of hair that has a curved shape.
The girl had long, black curls.

curtain *noun*
curtains

A **curtain** is a piece of cloth that you pull across a window to cover it.

curved *adjective*

If something is **curved**, it has the shape of a bent line.
The bird had a curved beak.

cushion *noun*
cushions

A **cushion** is a bag of soft material that you put on a seat to make it more comfortable.

customer *noun*
customers

A **customer** is a person who buys something in a shop.

cut *verb*
cuts, cutting, cut

1 If you **cut** something, you use a knife or scissors to divide it into pieces.
   Hello Kitty cut the cake.

2 If you **cut** yourself, something sharp goes through your skin and blood comes out.
   Don't cut yourself on the broken glass.

cut *noun*
cuts

A **cut** is a place on your skin where something sharp has gone through it.
He had a cut on his cheek.

Dd

dad or **daddy** *noun*
dads or **daddies**

Dad or **daddy** is a name for your father.

damage *verb*
damages, damaging, damaged

If you **damage** something, you break it or spoil it.
The storm damaged the roof.

damp *adjective*
damper, dampest

Something that is **damp** is a little bit wet.
Hello Kitty's hair was damp.

dance *verb*
dances, dancing, danced

When you **dance**, you move your body to music.

danger *noun*
dangers

If there is **danger**, something bad might happen to hurt you.
There is a danger that he will fall.

dangerous *adjective*

If something is **dangerous**, it can hurt you or kill you.
It is dangerous to cross the road here.

dark *adjective*
darker, darkest

1 When it is **dark**, there is no light or not much light.

2 A **dark** colour is not pale.
Hello Kitty wore a dark blue skirt.

date *noun*
dates

A **date** is the day, the month, and sometimes the year when something happens.
What date is your birthday, Hello Kitty?

daughter *noun*
daughters

Someone's **daughter** is their female child.

day *noun*
days

1 A **day** is the length of time between one midnight and the next. There are twenty-four hours in a **day**, and seven **days** in a week.
It is three days until Hello Kitty's birthday.

2 **Day** is the time when there is light outside.
Hello Kitty has been busy all day.

A B C D E F G H I J K L M N O P Q R S T U V W X Y Z

dead *adjective*

A person, an animal, or a plant that is **dead** has stopped living.

deaf *adjective*

Someone who is **deaf** cannot hear anything, or cannot hear very well.

December *noun*

December is the month after November and before January. It has 31 days.

decide *verb*
decides, deciding, decided

When you **decide** to do something, you think about it and then choose to do it.
*Hello Kitty **decided** to go home.*

decorate *verb*
decorates, decorating, decorated

If you **decorate** a room, you put paint or paper on its walls.
*We **decorated** the bedroom.*

deep *adjective*
deeper, deepest

If something is **deep**, it goes down a long way.
*Hello Kitty dug a **deep** hole in the sand.*

deer *noun*
deer

A **deer** is a large animal that lives in forests and can run very fast. Male **deer** have big horns that look like branches on their heads.

defend *verb*
defends, defending, defended

If you **defend** someone, you keep them safe from danger.
*The soldiers **defended** the king.*

delicious *adjective*

If food is **delicious**, it tastes or smells very good.

deliver *verb*
delivers, delivering, delivered

If you **deliver** something, you take it to someone.
*Please **deliver** this letter to him.*

dentist
dentists *noun*

A **dentist** is a person whose job is to take care of people's teeth.

depth *noun*
depths

The **depth** of something is how far down it goes from its top to its bottom.
*The **depth** of the pond is two metres.*

describe *verb*
describes, describing, described

If you **describe** something, you say what it is like.
*The teacher **described** the picture to the class.*

desert *noun*
deserts

A **desert** is a large, dry area of land with almost no trees or plants. **Deserts** are very hot and are often covered with sand.

desk *noun*
desks

A **desk** is a kind of table that you sit at to write or to work.

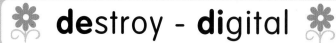

destroy *verb*
destroys, destroying, destroyed

If you **destroy** something, you damage it so much that it cannot be used any more.
*The fire **destroyed** the house.*

diagram *noun*
diagrams

A **diagram** is a drawing that shows something in a way that is very easy to understand.
*He drew me a **diagram** of the engine.*

diamond *noun*
diamonds

1 A **diamond** is a kind of jewel that is hard, clear, and shiny.

2 A **diamond** is also a shape with four straight sides.

diary *noun*
diaries

A **diary** is a book that you use to write down things that happen to you each day.

dice *noun*
dice

A **dice** is a small cube with a different number of spots on each side. You throw **dice** in some games.

dictionary *noun*
dictionaries

A **dictionary** is a book with a list of words in it. The **dictionary** tells you what these words mean, and shows you how to spell them.

did

♥ Look at **do**
*Hello Kitty saw what he **did**.*

didn't

Didn't is short for **did not**.
*Hello Kitty **didn't** like the film.*

die *verb*
dies, dying, died

When a person, an animal, or a plant **dies**, they stop living.
*Plants **die** if you don't water them.*

different *adjective*

If two things are **different**, they are not like each other.
*Hello Kitty's crayons were all in **different** colours.*

difficult *adjective*

If something is **difficult**, it is not easy to do or to understand.
*The homework was too **difficult** for us.*

dig *verb*
digs, digging, dug

If you **dig**, you make a hole in the ground.
*Hello Kitty **dug** a hole in the garden.*

digital *adjective*

If a machine is **digital**, it shows or sends information by using numbers.
*We have a new **digital** television.*

A B C D E F G H I J K L M N O P Q R S T U V W X Y Z

dinner - disk

dinner *noun*
dinners

Dinner is the main meal of the day.

dinosaur *noun*
dinosaurs

Dinosaurs were large animals that lived a very long time ago. **Dinosaurs** were like very big lizards.

direction *noun*
directions

1   A **direction** is the way that you go to get to a place.
    *Hello Kitty's house is in this **direction**.*

2   **Directions** are words or pictures that show you how to do something, or how to get somewhere.
    *He gave me **directions** to the station.*

dirt *noun*

Dirt is anything that is not clean, for example, dust or mud.
*She had **dirt** on her face.*

dirty *adjective*
dirtier, dirtiest

If something is **dirty**, it has mud, food, or other marks on it.
*The dishes were **dirty**.*

disappear *verb*
disappears, disappearing, disappeared

If something **disappears**, you cannot see it any more.
*The cat **disappeared** under the bed.*

disappointed *adjective*

If you are **disappointed**, you are sad because something you hoped for did not happen.
*I was **disappointed** that Hello Kitty wasn't there.*

disaster *noun*
disasters

A **disaster** is something very bad that happens suddenly and that may hurt many people.

discover *verb*
discovers, discovering, discovered

When you **discover** something, you get to know about it for the first time.
*We **discovered** that he was very good at football.*

discuss *verb*
discusses, discussing, discussed

When people **discuss** something, they talk about it together.
*We **discussed** what to do next.*

disease *noun*
diseases

A **disease** is something that makes you ill.
*Measles is a **disease**.*

disguise *noun*
disguises

A **disguise** is something you wear so that people will not know who you are.

dish *noun*
dishes

A **dish** is a container that you use to cook or serve food in.

disk *noun*
disks

A **disk** is a flat piece of metal and plastic that you use in a computer to store information.

a
b
c
d
e
f
g
h
i
j
k
l
m
n
o
p
q
r
s
t
u
v
w
x
y
z

37

A
B
C
D ❀
E
F
G
H
I
J
K
L
M
N
O
P
Q
R
S
T
U
V
W
X
Y
Z

distance *noun*
distances

The **distance** between two things is how much space there is between them.
Hello Kitty measured the distance between the wall and the table.

dive *verb*
dives, diving, dived

If you **dive** into water, you jump in so that your arms and your head go in first.

divide *verb*
divides, dividing, divided

1 If you **divide** something, you make it into smaller pieces.
   Divide the cake into four pieces.

2 When you **divide** numbers, you see how many times one number goes into another number.
   If you divide ten by five, you get two.

do *verb*
does, doing, did, done

If you **do** something, you spend some time on it or finish it.
Hello Kitty wanted to do her homework.

doctor *noun*
doctors

A **doctor** is a person whose job is to help people who are ill or hurt to get better.

does

🖤 Look at **do**
Hello Kitty always does her homework before dinner.

doesn't

Doesn't is short for **does not**.
He doesn't like carrots.

dog *noun*
dogs

A **dog** is an animal that barks. Some **dogs** do special jobs, like helping blind people.

doing

🖤 Look at **do**
What are you doing?

doll *noun*
dolls

A **doll** is a toy that looks like a small person or a baby.

dolphin *noun*
dolphins

A **dolphin** is an animal that lives in the sea and looks like a large fish with a long nose.
Dolphins are very clever.

done

🖤 Look at **do**
Hello Kitty has done a drawing.

donkey *noun*
donkeys

A **donkey** is an animal that looks like a small horse with long ears.

don't

Don't is short for **do not**.
I don't feel well.

door *noun*
doors

You open and close a **door** to get into a building, a room, or a cupboard.

double *adjective*

Double means two times as big, or two times as much.
His room is double the size of mine.

down

When something moves **down**, it goes from a higher place to a lower place.
Hello Kitty came down the stairs.

drag *verb*
drags, dragging, dragged

If you **drag** something, you pull it along the ground.
Hello Kitty dragged her chair to the table.

dragon *noun*
dragons

In stories, a **dragon** is a monster that has wings and can make fire come out of its mouth.

drain *verb*
drains, draining, drained

If you **drain** a liquid, you take it away by making it flow to another place.
They drained the water out of the tunnel.

drank

♥ Look at **drink**
The little girl drank a glass of water.

draw *verb*
draws, drawing, drew, drawn

When you **draw**, you use pens, pencils, or crayons to make a picture.
Hello Kitty likes to draw animals.

drawer *noun*
drawers

A **drawer** is a box that fits inside a piece of furniture. You can pull it out and put things in it.

drawing *noun*
drawings

A **drawing** is a picture you make with pens, pencils, or crayons.

drawn

♥ Look at **draw**
Hello Kitty has drawn her house.

dream *noun*
dreams

A **dream** is something you see and hear in your mind while you are sleeping.
Hello Kitty had a dream about winning the prize.

dress *noun*
dresses

A **dress** is something a girl or a woman can wear. It covers the body and part of the legs.
Hello Kitty wore a yellow dress.

dress *verb*
dresses, dressing, dressed

When you **dress**, you put on clothes.
*Hello Kitty **dressed** quickly because she was late.*

drew

🖤 Look at **draw**
*Hello Kitty **drew** a picture of a horse.*

drink *verb*
drinks, drinking, drank, drunk

When you **drink**, you swallow liquid.
*Mum **drinks** a lot of coffee.*

drip *verb*
drips, dripping, dripped

When liquid **drips**, a small amount of it falls from somewhere.
*Water **dripped** from the roof.*

drive *verb*
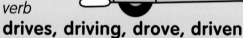
drives, driving, drove, driven

When someone **drives** a vehicle, they make it go where they want.
*He knows how to **drive** a car.*

drop *verb*
drops, dropping, dropped

If you **drop** something, you let it fall.
*Hello Kitty **dropped** a plate on the floor.*

drove

🖤 Look at **drive**
*We **drove** to the shops.*

drown *verb*
drowns, drowning, drowned

If someone **drowns**, they die because their face is below water and they cannot breathe.

drum *noun*
drums

A **drum** is an instrument that you hit with sticks or with your hands to make music.

drunk

🖤 Look at **drink**
*Dad has **drunk** all his milk.*

dry *adjective*
drier, driest

If something is **dry**, there is no water in it or on it.
*Hello Kitty's shoes are **dry** now.*

duck *noun*
ducks

A **duck** is a bird that lives near water and can swim. **Ducks** have large flat beaks.

dug

🖤 Look at **dig**
*Hello Kitty **dug** a hole in the sand.*

dull *adjective*
duller, dullest

1 Something that is **dull** is not interesting.
   *That was a very **dull** book.*

2 A **dull** colour is not bright.
   *He wore a **dull** green jacket.*

dust *noun*

Dust is tiny pieces of dry dirt that looks like powder.
*The table was covered in **dust**.*

Ee

a b c d **e** f g h i j k l m n o p q r s t u v w x y z

each

Each means every one.
Hello Kitty gave each of us a sweet.

eagle *noun*
eagles

An **eagle** is a large bird with a curved beak and sharp claws. **Eagles** eat small animals.

ear *noun*
ears

Your **ears** are the two parts of your body that you hear sounds with.
He whispered something in her ear.

early *adjective*
earlier, earliest

1   If you are **early**, you arrive before the time that you were expected to come.
She was too early for the party.

2   **Early** also means near the first part of something.
Hello Kitty got up early in the morning.

earn *verb*
earns, earning, earned

If you **earn** money, you work to get it.
He earned some money washing the car.

earth *noun*

1   The **Earth** is the planet that we live on.

2   **Earth** is also the soil that plants grow in.

earthquake *noun*
earthquakes

When there is an **earthquake**, the ground shakes and buildings often fall down.

east *noun*

The **east** is the direction that is in front of you when you are looking towards the place where the sun rises.

easy *adjective*
easier, easiest

If something is **easy**, you can do it or understand it without having to try very much.
Hello Kitty thinks these sums are easy.

eat *verb*
eats, eating, ate, eaten

When you **eat**, you chew and swallow food.
She eats too many sweets.

echo *noun*
echoes

An **echo** is a sound that you hear again because it bounces off something solid and then comes back.
Hello Kitty heard the echo of my voice in the cave.

edge *noun*
edges

The **edge** of something is the part along the end or side of it.
*Hello Kitty stood at the **edge** of the pond.*

effect *noun*
effects

An **effect** is something that happens because of another thing.
*The flood was an **effect** of all the rain.*

effort *noun*
efforts

If you make an **effort** to do something, you have to work a lot to do it.
*Hello Kitty made an **effort** to win the race.*

egg *noun*
eggs

Baby birds, insects, and some other animals live in **eggs** until they are big enough to come out and be born.
People often eat hens' **eggs** as food.

eight *noun*

Eight is the number **8**.

elbow *noun*
elbows

Your **elbow** is the part in the middle of your arm where it bends.
*She put her **elbows** on the table.*

electricity *noun*

Electricity is a kind of energy that is used to make light, to make things hot, and to make machines work.

elephant *noun*
elephants

An **elephant** is a very large, grey animal with big ears, a long nose called a trunk, and two long, curved teeth called tusks.

eleven *noun*

Eleven is the number **11**.

email *or* e-mail *noun*

An **email** is a message like a letter that you send from one computer to another.
*Hello Kitty got an **email** from her cousin.*

empty *adjective*
emptier, emptiest

If something is **empty**, there is nothing inside it.
*The bottle was **empty**.*

encyclopedia *noun*
encyclopedias

An **encyclopedia** is a book that gives you information about many different things.

end *noun*
ends

The **end** of something is the last part of it.
*Hello Kitty wanted to hear the **end** of the story.*

enemy *noun*
enemies

If someone is your **enemy**, they hate you and want to hurt you.

energy *noun*

1 If you have **energy**, you have the strength to move around a lot and do things.
*He has the **energy** to run for miles.*

2 **Energy** is also the power that makes machines work.
*The lamp gets its **energy** from the sun.*

engine *noun*
engines

1 An **engine** is a machine that makes things like cars and planes move.

2 An **engine** is also the front part of a train that pulls it along.

enjoy *verb*
enjoys, enjoying, enjoyed

If you **enjoy** something, you like doing it.
*Hello Kitty **enjoys** reading.*

enormous *adjective*

Something that is **enormous** is very big.
*Whales are **enormous**.*

enough

If you have **enough** of something, you have as much as you need.
*Hello Kitty has **enough** paper for two drawings.*

enter *verb*
enters, entering, entered

When you **enter** a place, you go into it.

entrance *noun*
entrances

The **entrance** of a place is the way you get into it.
*Hello Kitty found the **entrance** to the tunnel.*

envelope *noun*
envelopes

An **envelope** is a paper cover that you put a letter or a card into before you send it to someone.

environment *noun*

The **environment** is the land, water, and air around us.
*We must try to protect the **environment**.*

equal *adjective*

If two things are **equal**, they are the same in size, number, or amount.
*Mix **equal** amounts of milk and water.*

equipment *noun*

Equipment is all the things that you need to do something.
*He put his football **equipment** in his bag.*

escape *verb*
escapes, escaping, escaped

If a person or an animal **escapes**, they get away from somewhere.
*My guinea pig **escaped** from its cage.*

even *adjective*

1 An **even** number is a number that you can divide by two, with nothing left over.
*Four is an **even** number.*

2 Something that is **even** is flat and smooth.
*The path was straight and **even**.*

evening *noun*
evenings

The **evening** is the part of
each day between the end of the
afternoon and the time when people usually go to bed.

ever

Ever means at any time.
*Have you **ever** seen anything like it?*

every *adjective*

You use **every** to mean all the people or things
in a group.
Every pupil in Hello Kitty's school was there.

everybody

Everybody means all the people in a group, or
all the people in the world.
Everybody likes Hello Kitty.

everyone

Everyone means all the people in a group, or all
the people in the world.
Everyone knows who Hello Kitty is.

everything

Everything means all of something.
*I told Hello Kitty **everything** that happened.*

everywhere

Everywhere means in every place.
*Hello Kitty looked **everywhere** for her ball.*

example *noun*
examples

An **example** is something
that you use to show what
other things in the same
group are like.
*Here is an **example**
of Hello Kitty's
drawings.*

excellent *adjective*

Something that is **excellent** is very good.
*Hello Kitty thought it was an **excellent** film.*

excited *adjective*

If you are **excited**, you are very happy about
something and you keep thinking about it.
*Hello Kitty is **excited** about going to the beach.*

excuse *noun*
excuses

An **excuse** is a reason that you give to explain
why you did something.
*Hello Kitty had a good **excuse** for being late.*

exercise *noun*
exercises

1   When you do **exercise**, you
    move your body so that you
    can keep healthy and strong.
    *Playing tennis is good **exercise**.*

2   An **exercise** is also something you
    do to practise what you have learnt.
    *Hello Kitty did a maths **exercise**.*

exit *noun*
exits

The **exit** of a building is the door you use
to get out of it.
*Hello Kitty left by the nearest **exit**.*

A B C D E F G H I J K L M N O P Q R S T U V W X Y Z

expect verb
expects, expecting, expected

If you **expect** something to happen, you think that it will happen.
*Hello Kitty **expects** that he will come.*

expensive adjective

If something is **expensive**, you need a lot of money to buy it.

explain verb
explains, explaining, explained

If you **explain** something, you talk about it so that people can understand it.
*He **explained** to me how the machine worked.*

explode verb
explodes, exploding, exploded

If something **explodes**, it bursts with a very loud noise.

explore verb
explores, exploring, explored

If you **explore** a place, you look around it to see what it is like.
*Hello Kitty **explored** the old castle.*

extinct adjective

If an animal or a plant is **extinct**, there are none of them alive any more.
*Dinosaurs are **extinct**.*

extra adjective

Extra means more than the usual amount.
*Hello Kitty wore an **extra** jumper because it was cold.*

eye noun
eyes

Your **eyes** are the parts of your body that you see with.
*Hello Kitty opened her **eyes** and looked.*

Ff

face noun
faces

Your **face** is the front part of your head.
*She has a beautiful **face**.*

fact noun
facts

A **fact** is something that you know is true.

factory noun
factories

A **factory** is a large building where people use machines to make things.
*He works in a **factory** that makes computers.*

fail verb
fails, failing, failed

If you **fail**, you try to do something but you cannot do it.
*She **failed** to find her lost keys.*

fair adjective
fairer, fairest

1 If something is **fair**, it seems right because it is the same for everyone.
*It's not **fair** - he's got more than me!*

2 **Fair** hair is pale yellow in colour.

A
B
C
D
E
F
G
H
I
J
K
L
M
N
O
P
Q
R
S
T
U
V
W
X
Y
Z

fairy *noun*
fairies

In stories, **fairies** are tiny creatures with wings who can do magic.

fall *verb*
falls, falling, fell, fallen

If a person or thing **falls**, they move towards the ground suddenly by accident.
*He **fell** off his bike.*

fallen

♥ Look at **fall**
*An apple had **fallen** from the tree in Hello Kitty's garden.*

family *noun*
families

A **family** is a group of people made up of parents and their children. Aunts and uncles, cousins, grandmothers, and grandfathers are also part of your **family**.

famous *adjective*

If someone is **famous**, a lot of people know who they are.
*She wants to be rich and **famous**.*

far
farther, farthest

If something is **far** away, it is a long way away.
*His house was **far** away from Hello Kitty's.*

farm *noun*
farms

A **farm** is a piece of land with buildings on it where people grow crops and keep animals.

 farmer *noun*
farmers

A **farmer** is a person who grows crops and keeps animals on a farm.

fast *adjective*
faster, fastest

Something that is **fast** can move quickly.
*This car is very **fast**.*

fasten *verb*
fastens, fastening, fastened

When you **fasten** something, you close it up.
*Hello Kitty **fastened** the buttons on her coat.*

fat *adjective*
fatter, fattest

Someone who is **fat** has a big, round body.

father *noun*
fathers

A **father** is a man who has a child.

FRESH CORN

fault *noun*
faults

If something bad is your **fault**, you made it happen.
*It's my **fault** that we were late.*

favourite *adjective*

Your **favourite** person or thing is the one you like best.
*Hello Kitty's **favourite** food is melon.*

fear *noun*

Fear is the way you feel when you think that something bad is going to happen to you.
*She shook with **fear**.*

feast *noun*
feasts

A **feast** is a large and special meal for a lot of people.

feather *noun*
feathers

Feathers are the soft, light things that cover a bird's body. They keep the bird warm and help it to fly.

February *noun*

February is the month after January and before March. It usually has 28 days, but once every four years, it has 29 days.

feed *verb*
feeds, feeding, fed

If you **feed** a person or an animal, you give them food.
*Hello Kitty **feeds** her cat twice a day.*

feel *verb*
feels, feeling, felt

1 The way you **feel**, for example happy or sad, or cold or tired, is how you are at the time.
*I **feel** very upset.*

2 If you **feel** something, you touch it with your hand to see what it is like.
Feel how soft these feathers are.

feet

💜 Look at **foot**
*Don't put your **feet** on the chair.*

fell

💜 Look at **fall**
*She **fell** and hurt her knee.*

felt

💜 Look at **feel**
*I **felt** angry.*

female *adjective*

A **female** person or animal could become a mother.

fence *noun*
fences

A **fence** is a wall made of wood or metal that goes round a piece of land.
*There is a **fence** round Hello Kitty's garden.*

fetch *verb*
fetches, fetching, fetched

If you **fetch** something, you go to where it is and bring it back.
*Hello Kitty **fetched** a towel from the bathroom.*

fever *noun*
fevers

If you have a **fever** when you are ill, your body is too hot.

few
fewer, fewest

A **few** means some, but not many.
*She gave Hello Kitty a **few** cherries.*

field *noun*
fields

A **field** is a piece of land where people grow crops or keep animals.

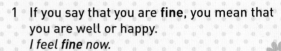

fierce *adjective*
fiercer, fiercest

A **fierce** animal is very angry and might attack you.
*That dog looks very **fierce**.*

fight *verb*
fights, fighting, fought

When people **fight**, they try to hurt each other.
*Two boys started to **fight** in the playground.*

fill *verb*
fills, filling, filled

If you **fill** something, you put so much into it that you cannot get any more in.
*Hello Kitty **filled** her glass with lemonade.*

film *noun*
films

A **film** is a story told in moving pictures that you watch on a screen.

fin *noun*
fins

A **fin** is one of the thin, flat parts on a fish's body that help it to swim.

find *verb*
finds, finding, found

If you **find** something that has been lost, you see it after you have been looking for it.
*Hello Kitty can't **find** her shoes.*

fine *adjective*
finer, finest

1 If you say that you are **fine**, you mean that you are well or happy.
*I feel **fine** now.*

2 Something that is **fine** is very thin.
*She sewed the cloth with **fine** thread.*

3 When the weather is **fine**, it is dry and sunny.
*It is a **fine** day.*

finger *noun*
fingers

Your **fingers** are the long thin parts at the end of each hand.
*She put her new ring on her **finger**.*

finish *verb*
finishes, finishing, finished

When you **finish** something, you come to the end of it.
*Hello Kitty **finished** her homework.*

fire *noun*
fires

Fire is the hot, bright flames that come from something that is burning.
*The **fire** destroyed the forest.*

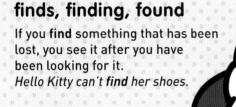

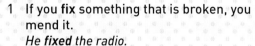

fire engine - flies

fire engine *noun*
fire engines

A **fire engine** is a large truck that carries people and equipment to stop fires.

firework *noun*
fireworks

Fireworks are things that make a loud bang or flashes of bright colour when they are burned.

firm *adjective*
firmer, firmest

Something that is **firm** is hard, and is not easy to bend.

first *adjective*

If a person or thing is **first**, they come before all the others.
*January is the **first** month of the year.*

fish *noun*
fish or **fishes**

A **fish** is an animal that lives in water.
Fish have fins to help them swim.

fit *verb*
fits, fitting, fitted

If something **fits** you, it is the right size and shape for you.
*These shoes don't **fit** me.*

five *noun*

Five is the number **5**.

fix *verb*
fixes, fixing, fixed

1 If you **fix** something that is broken, you mend it.
*He **fixed** the radio.*

2 If you **fix** something to another thing, you join them together.
*She **fixed** the shelf to the wall.*

flag *noun*
flags

A **flag** is a piece of cloth with a pattern on it. Each country of the world has its own **flag**.

flame *noun*
flames

A **flame** is the hot, bright light that comes from a fire.
*The **flames** almost burned her fingers.*

flash *noun*
flashes

A **flash** is a sudden bright light.
*There was a **flash** of lightning.*

flat *adjective*
flatter, flattest

If something is **flat**, it is smooth and does not have any lumps.
*Lay the painting on a **flat** surface until it is dry.*

flavour *noun*
flavours

The **flavour** of food is the taste that it has.
*They had ice cream in lots of **flavours**.*

flew

💜 Look at **fly**
*An aeroplane **flew** across the sky.*

flies

💜 Look at **fly**
*A bird **flies** by moving its wings.*

a
b
c
d
e
f
g
h
i
j
k
l
m
n
o
p
q
r
s
t
u
v
w
x
y
z

flock *noun*
flocks

A **flock** is the name for a group of birds or sheep.

flood *noun*
floods

If there is a **flood**, a lot of water covers land that is usually dry. *Hello Kitty couldn't get to school because of the flood.*

floor *noun*
floors

1 A **floor** is the part of a room that you walk on. *There were carpets on the floor.*

2 A **floor** of a building is all the rooms in it that are at the same height. *Our house is on the first floor.*

flour *noun*

Flour is a powder made from wheat that is used to make bread and cakes.

flow *verb*
flows, flowing, flowed

If something **flows**, it moves along in a steady way and does not stop. *The river flowed through the forest.*

flower *noun*
flowers

A **flower** is the part of a plant that makes seeds. **Flowers** often have bright colours and a nice smell.

flown

♥ Look at **fly**
The birds have all flown away.

flu *noun*

If you have **flu**, you feel as if you have a very bad cold, and your body aches.

fly *verb*
flies, flying, flew, flown

When a bird or aeroplane **flies**, it moves through the air.

fly *noun*
flies

A **fly** is a small insect with two thin, clear wings.

fog *noun*

Fog is a thick cloud that is close to the ground. It is hard to see through it.

fold *verb*
folds, folding, folded

If you **fold** something, you bend it so that one part of it goes over another. *Hello Kitty folded the letter and put it in the envelope.*

follow *verb*
follows, following, followed

If you **follow** someone, you go along behind them. *Hello Kitty followed him up the stairs.*

food *noun*
foods

Food is what people and animals eat.

foot *noun*
feet

Your **feet** are the parts of your body that are at the ends of your legs, and that you stand on.
*Hello Kitty was standing with one **foot** in front of the other.*

football *noun*
footballs

1 **Football** is a game played by two teams of eleven people who kick a ball and try to score goals by getting the ball into a net.

2 A **football** is the ball that you use to play football.

forehead *noun*
foreheads

Your **forehead** is the part of your face that is between your hair and your eyes.
*She had a bruise on her **forehead**.*

forest *noun*
forests

A **forest** is a place where a lot of trees grow close together.

forever

If something goes on **forever**, it never comes to an end.
*The film seemed to go on **forever**.*

forgave

💜 Look at **forgive**
*She **forgave** her brother for spoiling her drawing.*

forget *verb*
forgets, forgetting, forgot, forgotten

If you **forget** something, you do not remember it.
*Don't **forget** to lock the door.*

forgive *verb*
forgives, forgiving, forgave, forgiven

If you **forgive** someone who has done something bad, you stop being angry with them.
*Please **forgive** me for being late.*

forgot

💜 Look at **forget**
*Hello Kitty **forgot** to bring any money.*

forgotten

💜 Look at **forget**
*Hello Kitty has **forgotten** her bag.*

fork *noun*
forks

A **fork** is a tool with three or four thin, sharp points that you use to eat food with.

fortnight *noun*
fortnights

A **fortnight** is two weeks.

a b c d e **f** g h i j k l m n o p q r s t u v w x y z

A B C D E F G H I J K L M N O P Q R S T U V W X Y Z

forwards

If you move **forwards**, you move towards the front.
*Hello Kitty ran backwards and **forwards** trying to catch the ball.*

fought

♥ Look at **fight**
*The knights **fought** with swords.*

found

♥ Look at **find**
*Hello Kitty **found** a lost dog.*

four *noun*

Four is the number **4**.
*There were **four** apples.*

fox *noun*
foxes

A **fox** is an animal that looks like a dog with red fur and a long, thick tail.

fraction *noun*
fractions

A **fraction** is a part of a whole number.
*A half and a quarter are both **fractions**.*

frame *noun*
frames

A **frame** is a piece of wood, metal or plastic that fits around the edge of a picture, a window, or a door.

freckles *noun*

Freckles are light brown spots that some people have on their skin.
*His face was covered with **freckles**.*

free *adjective*
freer, freest

1 If something is **free**, you can have it without paying any money for it.
*If you buy a cup of coffee, you get a **free** cake.*

2 If you are **free**, you can do what you like or go where you like.
*You are **free** to come here any time.*

freeze *verb*
freezes, freezing, froze, frozen

1 When water **freezes**, it is so cold that it becomes ice.

2 If you **freeze** food, you make it very cold so that it will not go bad.

fresh *adjective*
fresher, freshest

1 If food is **fresh**, it has been picked or made a short time ago.
*She eats a piece of **fresh** fruit every day.*

2 **Fresh** water has no salt in it. The water in rivers is **fresh**.

3 **Fresh** air is clean and cool.

Friday *noun*
Fridays

Friday is the day after Thursday and before Saturday.
*Hello Kitty went home on **Friday**.*

fridge *noun*
fridges

A **fridge** is a cupboard that uses electricity to keep food cold and fresh.
*Hello Kitty put the milk in the **fridge**.*

fried

♥ Look at **fry**
*She **fried** some eggs.*

friend noun
friends

A **friend** is someone you know and like, and who likes you too.

friendly adjective
friendlier, friendliest

If someone is **friendly**, they like to meet other people, and are nice to them.

frighten verb
frightens, frightening, frightened

If something **frightens** you, it makes you feel afraid.
Loud noises frighten her.

frog noun
frogs

A **frog** is a small animal with smooth skin, big eyes, and long back legs that it uses for jumping. **Frogs** live near water.

front noun
fronts

The **front** of something is the part that comes first or the part that you usually see first.
Hello Kitty was at the front of the queue.

frost noun

Frost is ice that looks like white powder. It covers things outside when the weather is very cold.

frown verb
frowns, frowning, frowned

When you **frown**, lines appear on your forehead because you are cross or because you are thinking about something.

froze

💜 Look at **freeze**
It was so cold that the lake froze.

frozen

💜 Look at **freeze**
The water had frozen into ice.

fruit noun
fruits

Fruit is the part of a plant or a tree that has the seeds in it. You can eat many **fruits**, for example apples, bananas, and strawberries.

fry verb
fries, frying, fried

When you **fry** food, you cook it in hot oil or butter.
Fry the onions until they are brown.

a b c d e f g h i j k l m n o p q r s t u v w x y z

full *adjective*
fuller, fullest

If something is **full**, it has so much in it that it cannot hold any more.
*The bottle is **full**.*

fun *noun*

When you have **fun**, you enjoy doing something and you feel happy.
*Hello Kitty had **fun** at the beach.*

funny *adjective*
funnier, funniest

1   If something is **funny**, it makes you laugh.
*Hello Kitty thought the joke was very **funny**.*

2   **Funny** also means strange.
*The car is making a **funny** noise.*

fur *noun*

Fur is the soft hair that covers the bodies of many animals.
*Pandas have black and white **fur**.*

furniture *noun*

Furniture is the name for all the big things, for example tables, chairs, or beds, that people have in their houses.
*We bought new **furniture** for the bedroom.*

future *noun*

The **future** is the time that will come after the present time.
*In the **future**, people will travel to other planets.*

gale *noun*
gales

A **gale** is a very strong wind.

game *noun*
games

1   A **game** is something you play that has rules, for example football.

2   Children also play a **game** when they pretend to be other people.
*Hello Kitty played a **game** of pirates.*

gap *noun*
gaps

A **gap** is a space between two things.
*There was a **gap** between the curtains.*

garage *noun*
garages

1   A **garage** is a building where you keep a car.

2   A **garage** is also a place where you can get your car repaired.

garden *noun*
gardens

A **garden** is a piece of land near a house where people can grow grass, flowers, and vegetables.

gas *noun*
gases

A **gas** is anything, for example air, that is not solid or a liquid.

gate *noun*
gates

A **gate** is a kind of door in a wall, a fence, or a hedge.

gave

♥ Look at **give**
*Hello Kitty **gave** me a present.*

gentle *adjective*
gentler, gentlest

If you are **gentle**, you are careful and not rough.
*Hello Kitty was **gentle** when she held the baby.*

get *verb*
gets, getting, got

1 You can use **get** to mean the same as "become".
*We should go before it **gets** dark.*

2 If you **get** somewhere, you arrive there.
*Hello Kitty **got** home at noon.*

3 If you **get** something, someone gives it to you.
*Hello Kitty **got** a bike for her birthday.*

4 If you **get** something, you go to where it is and bring it back.
*Hello Kitty went to **get** an ice cream.*

ghost *noun*
ghosts

A **ghost** is a dead person who some people think they can see and hear.

giant *adjective*

Something that is **giant** is very large.
*Hello Kitty watched the film on a **giant** TV screen.*

giraffe *noun*
giraffes

A **giraffe** is a very tall animal with a long neck, long legs, and dark spots on its body.

girl *noun*
girls

A **girl** is a child or a young person who is a female.

give *verb*
gives, giving, gave, given

If you **give** someone something, you let them have it to keep.
*Hello Kitty always **gives** her mother flowers on her birthday.*

glad *adjective*
gladder, gladdest

If you are **glad**, you are happy about something.
*Hello Kitty is **glad** her friend can come to play.*

glass *noun*
glasses

1 **Glass** is a hard, clear material that is used to make things like windows and bottles.
*The salad was in a **glass** bowl.*

2 A **glass** is also a container made from **glass** that you can drink out of.
*Hello Kitty filled her **glass** with milk.*

glasses *noun*

Glasses are two pieces of plastic or glass in a frame that people wear in front of their eyes to help them to see better.

a
b
c
d
e
f
g
h
i
j
k
l
m
n
o
p
q
r
s
t
u
v
w
x
y
z

A B C D E F **G** H I J K L M N O P Q R S T U V W X Y Z

glove noun
gloves

Gloves are things that you wear over your hands to keep them warm. **Gloves** have one part for your thumb and one for all your fingers.

glue noun

You use **glue** to stick things together.

go verb
goes, going, went, gone

1 If you **go** somewhere, you move there from another place.
Can we go to the park?

2 If you say that something is **going** to happen, you mean that it will happen.
It's going to rain soon.

goal noun
goals

In games like football, the **goal** is the place that you try to get the ball into to score a point.

goat noun
goats

A **goat** is an animal about the size of a sheep. **Goats** have horns, and hair on their chin that looks like a beard.

gold noun

Gold is a valuable, yellow metal that is used to make things like rings and necklaces, and also coins.

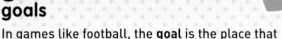

goldfish noun
goldfish

A **goldfish** is a small orange fish that people often keep as a pet.

gone

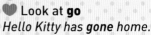 Look at **go**
Hello Kitty has gone home.

good adjective
better, best

1 If you say that something is **good**, you like it.
Hello Kitty thought it was a good film.

2 If you are **good**, you behave well.
Be good while I am out.

3 If you are **good** at something, you do it well.
Hello Kitty is good at drawing.

goodbye

You say **goodbye** to someone when one of you is going away.

good night

You say **good night** to someone late in the evening before you go home or go to bed.

goose noun
geese

A **goose** is a large bird with a long neck that lives near water.

gorilla noun
gorillas

A **gorilla** is a large, strong animal with long arms, black fur, and a black face.

got

 Look at **get**
They soon got tired of the game.

grain noun
grains

1 A **grain** is the seed of a cereal plant, for example rice or wheat.

2 A **grain** of something, for example sand or salt, is a tiny piece of it.

gram noun
grams

A **gram** is used for measuring how heavy things are.
There are about 400 grams of jam in this jar.

grandfather *noun*
grandfathers

Your **grandfather** is your father's father or your mother's father.

grandmother *noun*
grandmothers

Your **grandmother** is your father's mother or your mother's mother.

grape *noun*
grapes

A **grape** is a small, round, green or purple fruit that grows in bunches.

grapefruit *noun*
grapefruits

A **grapefruit** is a large, round, yellow fruit with a sour taste.

graph *noun*
graphs

In maths, a **graph** is a picture that uses lines or shapes to show numbers.

grass *noun*
grasses

Grass is a green plant with very thin leaves that cover the ground in fields and gardens.

great *adjective*
greater, greatest

1   **Great** means very large.
    *The king lived in a **great** palace.*

2   **Great** also means very important.
    *The computer was a **great** invention.*

3   If you say that something is **great**, you mean that it is very good.
    *Hello Kitty had a **great** time at the party.*

greedy *adjective*
greedier, greediest

If someone is **greedy**, they want to have more of something than they need.
*He was so **greedy** that he ate the whole cake.*

green *noun*

Green is the colour of grass or leaves.
*Hello Kitty's dress is **green**.*

grew

💜 Look at **grow**
*The tree **grew** to a great height.*

grey *noun*

Grey is a mixture of black and white, like the colour of clouds when rain is falling.

ground *noun*

The **ground** is the earth or other surface that you walk on outside.

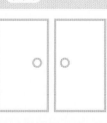

a
b
c
d
e
f
g
h
i
j
k
l
m
n
o
p
q
r
s
t
u
v
w
x
y
z

group *noun*
groups

A **group** is a number of people or things that are together, or that belong together.

grow *verb*
grows, growing, grew, grown

When something **grows**, it gets bigger.
*The puppy **grew** into a huge dog.*

guess *verb*
guesses, guessing, guessed

If you **guess**, you say what you think is true about something, but you do not really know if you are right.
*Can you **guess** how old he is?*

guinea pig *noun*
guinea pigs

A **guinea pig** is a small animal with fur and no tail that people often keep as a pet.

guitar *noun*
guitars

A **guitar** is an instrument with strings that you play by pressing the strings with one hand and pulling them with the other hand.

Hh

had

♥ Look at **have**
*Hello Kitty **had** a nice time.*

hadn't

Hadn't is short for **had not**.
*Hello Kitty **hadn't** seen them for a long time.*

hair *noun*

Hair is the soft, fine threads that grow on your head and on the bodies of many animals.
*I wash my **hair** every night.*

half *noun*
halves

A **half** is one of two equal parts that make up a whole thing.
*Hello Kitty had **half** of the cake.*

halves

♥ Look at **half**
*Cut the apples into **halves**.*

hamster *noun*
hamsters

A **hamster** is a small animal that looks like a fat mouse with a short tail. People often keep **hamsters** as pets.

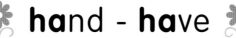
hand *noun*
hands

Your **hands** are the parts of your body that are at the ends of your arms, and that you use to hold things. A **hand** has four fingers and a thumb.
*Jody is wearing a glove on one **hand**.*

handle *noun*
handles

1 A **handle** is something that is joined to a door, a window, or a drawer, that you use to open and close it.
*Hello Kitty pulled the **handle** of the drawer.*

2 A **handle** is also the part of something, for example a tool or a bag, that you use to hold it.
*Hold the knife by its **handle**.*

hang *verb*
hangs, hanging, hung

If you **hang** something somewhere, you fix the top of it to something so that it does not touch the ground.
*You must **hang** your coat on a peg.*

happen *verb*
happens, happening, happened

When something **happens**, it takes place.
*What's **happening** in the playground?*

happy *adjective*
happier, happiest

When you are **happy**, you feel pleased about something.
*Hello Kitty is **happy** when she is dancing.*

hard *adjective*
harder, hardest

1 Something that is **hard** is solid, and it is not easy to bend it or break it.
*The glass broke on the **hard** floor.*

2 If something is **hard**, you have to try a lot to do it or to understand it.
*These sums are quite **hard**.*

has

💙 Look at **have**
*He **has** a sister.*

hasn't

Hasn't is short for **has not**.
*Hello Kitty **hasn't** anything to do.*

hat *noun*
hats

A **hat** is something that you can wear on your head.

hatch *verb*
hatches, hatching, hatched

When a baby bird or other animal **hatches**, it comes out of its egg by breaking the shell. You can also say that the egg **hatches**.

hate *verb*
hates, hating, hated

If you **hate** a person or a thing, you feel that you do not like them at all.
*I **hate** onions.*

have *verb*
has, having, had

1 If you **have** something, it belongs to you.
*Do you **have** any pets?*

2 When you **have** something, you feel it, or it happens to you.
*I **have** a bad cold.*

a b c d e f g **h** i j k l m n o p q r s t u v w x y z

59

haven't

Haven't is short for **have not**.
*I **haven't** any chocolate left.*

hay *noun*

Hay is dry grass that is used to feed animals.

head *noun*
heads

1   Your **head** is the part
    of your body at the top
    that has your eyes, ears,
    nose, mouth, and brain in it.
    *The ball hit him on the **head**.*

2   The **head** of something is the person
    who is its leader.
    *He is the **head** of the school.*

heal *verb*
heals, healing, healed

If something like a broken bone **heals**,
it gets better.

healthy *adjective*
healthier, healthiest

1   Someone who is **healthy** is well and strong
    and is not often ill.
    *People need exercise to stay **healthy**.*

2   Something that is **healthy** is good for you.
    *Hello Kitty loves **healthy** food like fruit.*

hear *verb*
hears, hearing, heard

When you **hear** a sound, you notice it through
your ears.
*Hello Kitty **heard** a dog barking.*

heart *noun*
hearts

Your **heart** is the part inside
you that makes the blood
move around your body.
*His **heart** was going fast.*

heavy *adjective*
heavier, heaviest

Something that is **heavy** weighs a lot.
*Hello Kitty's bag is very **heavy**.*

he'd

1   **He'd** is short for **he had**.
    ***He'd** seen it before.*

2   **He'd** is also short for **he would**.
    ***He'd** like them.*

A B C D E F G **H** I J K L M N O P Q R S T U V W X Y Z

hedge *noun*
hedges

A **hedge** is a row of bushes growing close together that makes a kind of wall. You often see **hedges** around fields.

heel *noun*
heels

Your **heels** are the parts of your feet at the back, below your ankles.
*He dragged his **heels** along the ground.*

height *noun*
heights

Your **height** is how tall you are.
*We all measured our **heights**.*

held

💜 Look at **hold**
*Mum **held** Hello Kitty's hand as they crossed the road.*

helicopter *noun*
helicopters

A **helicopter** is a small aircraft with long blades on top that go round very quickly. **Helicopters** can fly straight up and down and stay in one place in the air.

he'll

He'll is short for **he will**.
He'll come back soon.

hello

You say **hello** to someone when you meet them.

help *verb*
helps, helping, helped

If you **help** someone, you make it easier for them to do something.
*He **helped** Hello Kitty with her homework.*

hen *noun*
hens

A **hen** is a chicken that is a female. People often eat **hens'** eggs as food.

her

You use **her** to talk about a woman or a girl, or to say that something belongs to a woman or a girl.
*I gave **her** back **her** pen.*

herd *noun*
herds

A **herd** is a large group of animals that lives together.
*Hello Kitty saw a **herd** of deer in the forest.*

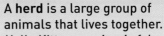

here

Here means the place where you are.
*Come and sit **here**.*

hers

You use **hers** to say that something belongs to a woman or a girl.
*Hello Kitty wondered which plate was **hers**.*

herself

You use **herself** when you want to say that something a woman or a girl does has an effect on her.
*Hello Kitty pulled **herself** out of the water.*

he's

He's is short for **he is**.
He's six years old.

hexagon *noun*
hexagons

A **hexagon** is a shape with six straight sides.

hid

💜 Look at **hide**
*Hello Kitty **hid** behind a chair.*

hidden

🖤 Look at **hide**

*Hello Kitty was **hidden** under the bed.*

hide *verb*
hides, hiding, hid, hidden

1 If you **hide** something, you put it where no one can see it or find it.
*Hello Kitty **hid** her bike behind the wall.*

2 If you **hide** what you feel, you do not let people know about it.
*She tried to **hide** how angry she was.*

high *adjective*
higher, highest

1 Something that is **high** is tall or is a long way above the ground.
*There was a **high** wall around the house.*

2 **High** also means great in amount or strength.
*They charged us a **high** price.*

3 A **high** sound or voice goes up a long way.
*She spoke in a **high** voice.*

hill *noun*
hills

A **hill** is a piece of land that is higher than the land around it. **Hills** are not as high as mountains.

him

You use **him** to talk about a man or a boy.
*Hello Kitty met **him** at the station.*

himself

You use **himself** when you want to say that something a man or a boy does has an effect on him.
*He fell and hurt **himself**.*

hippopotamus *noun*
hippopotamuses or hippopotami

A **hippopotamus** is a large animal with short legs and thick skin that lives near rivers.

his

You use **his** to say that something belongs to a man or a boy.
*He showed Hello Kitty **his** new ball.*

history *noun*

History is the story of what has happened in the past.

hit *verb*
hits, hitting, hit

If you **hit** something, you touch it with a lot of strength.
*Hello Kitty **hit** the ball with the bat.*

A B C D E F G H I J K L M N O P Q R S T U V W X Y Z

spf 30

hive *noun*
hives

A **hive** is a place where bees live.

hold *verb*
holds, holding, held

1 When you **hold** something, you have it in your hands or your arms.
Hello Kitty held the baby in her arms.

2 If something **holds** an amount of something, then that is how much it has room for inside.
The theatre holds 400 people.

hole *noun*
holes

A **hole** is a gap or a hollow place in something.
Hello Kitty dug a hole in the ground.

holiday *noun*
holidays

A **holiday** is a time when you do not need to work or go to school.

hollow *adjective*

Something that is **hollow** has an empty space inside it.
The owl's nest was in a hollow tree.

home *noun*
homes

Your **home** is the place where you live.
Hello Kitty stayed at home and watched TV.

homework *noun*

Homework is something like sums that a teacher gives you to work on at home.

honest *adjective*

If someone is **honest**, they do not tell lies, and you can believe what they say.

honey *noun*

Honey is a sweet, very thick liquid that is made by bees. You can eat **honey** on bread.

hoof *noun*
hooves

A **hoof** is the hard part of a horse's foot. Deer and cows also have **hooves**.

hop *verb*
hops, hopping, hopped

1 If you **hop**, you jump on one foot.

2 When animals or birds **hop**, they jump with two feet together.

hope *verb*
hopes, hoping, hoped

If you **hope** that something will happen, you want it to happen.
I hope you feel better soon.

horn *noun*
horns

1 A **horn** is one of the hard bones with sharp points that grow out of some animals' heads. Goats and bulls have **horns**.

2 A **horn** is also an instrument that you blow into to make music.

horrible *adjective*

If something is **horrible**, it is very nasty.
There was a horrible smell.

a
b
c
d
e
f
g
❀ **h**
i
j
k
l
m
n
o
p
q
r
s
t
u
v
w
x
y
z

horse *noun*
horses

A **horse** is a large animal with a long tail and four legs. People ride on **horses** or use them to pull things along.

hospital *noun*
hospitals

A **hospital** is a building where doctors and nurses care for people who are ill or hurt.

hot *adjective*
hotter, hottest

If something is **hot**, it is very warm.
*Don't touch the plate - it's **hot**.*

hour *noun*
hours

An **hour** is used for measuring time. There are sixty minutes in an **hour**, and twenty-four **hours** in a day.

house *noun*
houses

A **house** is a building where people live.
*Come to my **house** for dinner.*

how

1   You use the word **how** when you ask about the way that something happens or the way that you do something.
How do you spell your name?

2   You also use **how** when you ask about an amount.
How many people were at Hello Kitty's party?

hug *verb*
hugs, hugging, hugged

When you **hug** someone, you put your arms around them and hold them close to you.
*Hello Kitty **hugged** me as I said goodbye.*

huge *adjective*

Something that is **huge** is very big.
*Elephants are **huge** animals.*

human *adjective*

Something that is **human** is to do with people, and not animals or machines.
*There are over 200 bones in the **human** body.*

hundred *noun*

A **hundred** is the number **100**.

hung

♥ Look at **hang**
*He **hung** from the bars.*

hungry *adjective*
hungrier, hungriest

If you are **hungry**, you want to eat something.

hunt verb
hunts, hunting, hunted

1 When animals **hunt**, they chase another animal to kill it for food.
The lions hunted a zebra.

2 If you **hunt** for something, you try to find it.
Hello Kitty hunted for her new book.

hurry verb
hurries, hurrying, hurried

If you **hurry**, you move quickly or do something quickly.
We'll be late if we don't hurry.

hurt verb
hurts, hurting, hurt

If you **hurt** someone or something, you make them feel pain.
I fell over and hurt my leg yesterday.

husband noun
husbands

A woman's **husband** is the man she is married to.

hut noun
huts

A **hut** is a small building with one or two rooms. **Huts** are made of wood, mud, or grass.

hutch noun
hutches

A **hutch** is a kind of cage made of wood and wire, where people keep rabbits and other small pets.

I i

I

You use **I** to talk about yourself.
I like dogs.

ice noun

Ice is water that has frozen. It is very cold and hard.
The ground was covered with ice.

ice cream noun

Ice cream is a very cold, sweet food that is made from frozen milk or cream.

icicle noun
icicles

An **icicle** is a long piece of ice with a point at the end that hangs down from something. **Icicles** are made from dripping water that has frozen.

I'd

1 **I'd** is short for **I had**.
I'd been there before.

2 **I'd** is also short for **I would**.
I'd like to go to the zoo.

a b c d e f g h **i** j k l m n o p q r s t u v w x y z

A
B
C
D
E
F
G
H
I
J
K
L
M
N
O
P
Q
R
S
T
U
V
W
X
Y
Z

idea *noun*
ideas

An **idea** is something new that you have thought of.
*Hello Kitty had an **idea** for a story.*

ill *adjective*

When you are **ill**,
you do not feel well.
*She is too **ill** to go to school.*

I'll

I'll is short for **I will**.
I'll come back tomorrow.

illness *noun*
illnesses

If you have an **illness**, you do not feel well.
*He has just had a very bad **illness**.*

I'm

I'm is short for **I am**.
I'm hungry.

imagine *verb*
imagines, imagining, imagined

If you **imagine** something, you make a picture of
it in your mind.
Imagine that you are a cat.

immediately

If you do something **immediately**, you do it now.
*Stop that noise **immediately**!*

important *adjective*

1 If something is **important**, people care about
   it and think about it a lot.
   *Hello Kitty knows it is **important** not to tell lies.*

2 If someone is **important**, people pay a lot of
   attention to what they say and do.
   *She is a very **important** person.*

impossible *adjective*

If something is **impossible**, it cannot be done, or
it cannot happen.
*It is **impossible** to see in the dark.*

in

1 **In** means not outside.
   *The juice is **in** the fridge.*

2 You also use **in** to say when something
   happens.
   *Hello Kitty was born **in** November.*

inch *noun*
inches

An **inch** is used for measuring the length
of something. There are about two and half
centimetres in an **inch**.

indoors

If you are **indoors**, you are inside a building.

information *noun*

Information about something is facts that tell
you about it.
*I need some **information** about birds.*

ink *noun*

Ink is a liquid that you use to write or print with.
Pens have **ink** inside them.

insect *noun*
insects

An **insect** is a small animal with six legs, for
example a bee or a beetle. Many **insects** have
wings and can fly.

inside

1 If something is **inside** another thing, it is in it.
   *There was a letter **inside** the envelope.*

2 **Inside** also means indoors.
   *Hello Kitty went **inside** and sat down.*

instructions *noun*

Instructions are words or pictures that tell you how to do something.
*Here are the **instructions** for building the tent.*

instrument *noun*
instruments

1 An **instrument** is a tool that you use to do something. *The doctor used an **instrument** to look in Hello Kitty's ears.*

2 An **instrument** is also something, for example a piano or a guitar, that you use to make music. *He plays three **instruments**.*

intelligent *adjective*

If a person is **intelligent**, they are able to understand and learn things quickly.

interesting *adjective*

If something is **interesting**, you want to know more about it.

internet *noun*

The **internet** is something that joins a computer to other computers all over the world. You send emails using the **internet**.

interrupt *verb*
interrupts, interrupting, interrupted

If you **interrupt** someone, you say or do something that makes them stop in the middle of what they are doing.
*Don't **interrupt** the teacher when she's talking.*

invention *noun*
inventions

An **invention** is something that someone has made, and that nobody has ever thought of or made before.
*His new **invention** is a car that can fly.*

invisible *adjective*

If something is **invisible**, you cannot see it.

invite *verb*
invites, inviting, invited

If you **invite** someone to something, for example a party, you ask them to come to it.

iron *noun*
irons

1 **Iron** is a strong, hard, grey metal.

2 An **iron** is a piece of equipment with a flat bottom that gets hot. You move the **iron** over clothes to make them smooth.

is
💜 Look at **be**
She is six years old.

island *noun*
islands

An **island** is a piece of land that has water all around it.

isn't
Isn't is short for **is not**.
He isn't very happy.

it
You use **it** to talk about a thing or an animal.
This is a good book - have you read it?

its
You use **its** to say that something belongs to a thing or an animal.
The lion lifted its head.

it's
It's is short for **it is**.
It's one o'clock.

I've
I've is short for **I have**.
I've been playing football.

J j

jacket *noun*
jackets

A **jacket** is a short coat.

jam *noun*
Jam is a soft, sweet food that is made from fruit and sugar.
Hello Kitty loves strawberry jam on her bread.

January *noun*
January is the month after December and before February. It has 31 days.

jar *noun*
jars

A **jar** is a glass container with a lid that is used for storing food.
Make sure you put the lid back on the jar.

jaw *noun*
jaws

Your **jaws** are the top and bottom bones of your mouth.

jeans *noun*
Jeans are blue trousers with pockets at the front and back.
Everyone on the trip wore jeans and a bright T-shirt.

jelly *noun*

Jelly is a clear, sweet food that is solid but soft.
*At the party there was birthday cake, then **jelly** and ice cream.*

jet *noun*
jets

A **jet** is a plane that flies very fast.

jewel *noun*
jewels

1 A **jewel** is a valuable stone, like a diamond.
2 **Jewels** are things made with valuable stones, that you wear to decorate your body.
*She put the **jewels** in the box and turned the key.*

jigsaw *noun*
jigsaws

A **jigsaw** is a picture on cardboard that has been cut up into pieces. You have to fit them together again.
*Hello Kitty put the last pieces in the **jigsaw**.*

job *noun*
jobs

A **job** is the work that a person does to earn money.
*My sister wants to get a **job**.*

join *verb*
joins, joining, joined

1 If you **join** a group of people, you become one of the group.
*Come and **join** the music group after school on Mondays.*

2 When things **join**, or you **join** them, they come together.
*They **joined** hands and danced.*

joke *noun*
jokes

A **joke** is something that someone says to make you laugh.
*Grandfather always tells us **jokes** after dinner.*

journey *noun*
journeys

When you make a **journey**, you travel from one place to another.
*It was a difficult **journey** that took several days.*

jug *noun*
jugs

A **jug** is a container with a handle.
You use a **jug** for pouring liquids.
*There is a **jug** of cold water on the table.*

juice *noun*
juices

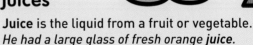

Juice is the liquid from a fruit or vegetable.
*He had a large glass of fresh orange **juice**.*

July *noun*

July is the month after June and before August. It has 31 days.

jump *verb*
jumps, jumping, jumped

When you **jump**, you bend your knees and push yourself into the air.
*Hello Kitty **jumped** over the fence.*

jumper *noun*
jumpers

You wear a **jumper** to keep yourself warm. It has sleeves and covers the top half of your body.

June *noun*

June is the month after May and before July. It has 30 days.

jungle *noun*
jungles

A **jungle** is a thick, wet forest in a hot country.
*They followed the path deep into the **jungle**.*

just

If you **just** did something, you did it a very short time ago.
*Hello Kitty **just** got home from school.*

Kk

kangaroo *noun*
kangaroos

A **kangaroo** is a large Australian animal that carries its babies in a pocket on its stomach.

keen *adjective*
keener, keenest

If you are **keen**, you want to do something very much.
*Hello Kitty was **keen** to help.*

keep *verb*
keeps, keeping, kept

1 If someone **keeps** away from a place, they do not go near it.
   ***Keep** away from the road.*

2 If someone **keeps** still or warm, they stay like that.
   *We lit a fire to **keep** warm.*
   *"**Keep** still!"*

3 If you **keep** doing something, you do it many times or you do it some more.
   *I **keep** forgetting to take my umbrella.*

4 When you **keep** something, you store it somewhere.
   *Hello Kitty **keeps** her books on a shelf.*

kennel - kitchen

kennel *noun*
kennels

A **kennel** is a small house where a dog can sleep.

kept

♥ Look at **keep**
Hello Kitty kept her bedroom tidy.

kettle *noun*
kettles

A **kettle** is a metal container with a lid and a handle, that you use for boiling water.
Mum put the kettle on and made some tea.

key *noun*
keys

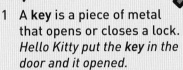

1 A **key** is a piece of metal that opens or closes a lock.
Hello Kitty put the key in the door and it opened.

2 The **keys** on a computer or instrument are the buttons that you press on it.
Press the "Enter" key.

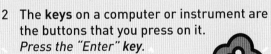

kick *verb*
kicks, kicking, kicked

If you **kick** something, you hit it with your foot.
Hello Kitty kicked the ball really hard.

kid *noun*
kids

A **kid** is a child.
They have three kids.

kill *verb*
kills, killing, killed

To **kill** a living thing is to make it die.
The earthquake killed 62 people.

kilogram *noun*
kilograms

A **kilogram** is used for measuring how heavy things are. There are 1000 grams in a **kilogram**.
The box weighs 4.5 kilograms.

kilometre *noun*
kilometres

A **kilometre** is used for measuring distance. There are 1000 metres in a **kilometre**, which is about 0.62 miles.

kind *noun*
kinds

A **kind** of thing is a type or sort of that thing.
What kind of car is that?

kind *adjective*
kinder, kindest

Someone who is **kind** is friendly and helps you.
Thank you for being so kind to me.

king *noun*
kings

A **king** is a man who rules a country.
Hello Kitty saw the king and queen arriving.

kiss *verb*
kisses, kissing, kissed

If you **kiss** someone, you touch them with your lips.
We kissed goodbye at the airport.

kitchen *noun*
kitchens

A **kitchen** is a room that is used for cooking.

a b c d e f g h i j **k** l m n o p q r s t u v w x y z

71

A B C D E F G H I J K L M N O P Q R S T U V W X Y Z

kite noun
kites

A **kite** is a toy that you fly in the wind at the end of a long string.
Hello Kitty went to the beach to fly her kite.

kitten noun
kittens

A **kitten** is a very young cat.

knee noun
knees

Your **knee** is the part in the middle of your leg where it bends.
I fell over and hurt my knee.

kneel verb
kneels, kneeling, knelt

When you **kneel**, you bend your legs and rest on one or both of your knees.
Hello Kitty knelt down beside the bed.

knew

♥ Look at **know**
Hello Kitty knew all the kids at the party.

knife noun
knives

A **knife** is a sharp metal tool that you use to cut things.
I always eat dinner with a knife and fork.

knight noun
knights

In the past, a **knight** was a soldier who rode a horse.

knit verb
knits, knitting, knitted

If you **knit** something, you make it from a long piece of wool by using two special sticks.
Hello Kitty's grandmother sat knitting.

knives

♥ Look at **knife**
We put all the knives away in their box.

knock verb
knocks, knocking, knocked

If you **knock** on something, you hit it to make a noise.
Hello Kitty went to his house and knocked on the door.

knot noun
knots

You make a **knot** when you tie two pieces of something together.
Hello Kitty picked up the rope and tied a knot in it.

know verb
knows, knowing, knew, known

1 If you **know** something, you have that information in your mind.
You should know the answer to that question.

2 If you **know** a person, you have met them and spoken to them.
Hello Kitty didn't know any of the other people in the class.

Ll

ladybird *noun*
ladybirds

A **ladybird** is a small round beetle that has red wings with black spots.

laid

♥ Look at **lay**
Hello Kitty laid out the food on the table.

lain

♥ Look at **lie**
He had lain awake all night, worrying.

lake *noun*
lakes

A **lake** is an area of water with land around it.

lamb *noun*
lambs

A **lamb** is a young sheep.

lamp *noun*
lamps

A **lamp** is a light that uses electricity, oil or gas.
Hello Kitty turned on the lamp by her bed.

land *noun*

Land is an area of ground.
This is good farm land.

land *verb*
lands, landing, landed

When something **lands**, it comes down to the ground after moving through the air.
Hello Kitty's ball landed on the grass.

lane *noun*
lanes

A **lane** is a narrow road, usually in the country.

label *noun*
labels

A **label** is a small note on something that gives you information about it.
The prices are on the labels.

lace *noun*
laces

1 **Lace** is a pretty cloth that has patterns of holes in it.
Hello Kitty's dress was blue with a white lace collar.

2 **Laces** are like pieces of string for fastening shoes.
Hello Kitty put on her shoes and tied the laces.

ladder *noun*
ladders

A **ladder** is a set of steps that you can move around. You use it for reaching high places.
Hello Kitty climbed the ladder to see over the wall.

lady *noun*
ladies

You can use **lady** to talk about a woman in a polite way.
She's a very nice old lady.

A B C D E F G H I J K L M N O P Q R S T U V W X Y Z

language *noun*
languages

A **language** is a set of words that the people of a country use in talking or writing.
The English language has over 500,000 words.

lap *noun*
laps

Your **lap** is the flat area on top of your thighs when you are sitting down.
Hello Kitty sat on her mum's lap.

large *adjective*
larger, largest

A **large** thing or person is big or bigger than usual.
This fish lives in large rivers and lakes.

last *adjective*

1   The **last** thing is the one before this one.
    In the last lesson, we looked at some flowers.

2   The **last** thing or person comes after all the others.
    Hello Kitty read the last three pages of the chapter.

late
later, latest

1   **Late** means near the end of a period of time.
    It was late in the afternoon.

2   **Late** also means after the proper time.
    We arrived late for our class.

laugh *verb*
laughs, laughing, laughed

When you **laugh**, you smile and make a sound because something is funny.
She laughed at the joke.

law *noun*
laws

A **law** is a rule that tells people what they may or may not do in a country.

lawn *noun*
lawns

A **lawn** is an area of short grass.
Hello Kitty is sitting on the lawn.

lay *verb*
lays, laying, laid

1   When you **lay** something somewhere, you put it down so that it lies there.
    Lay the dishes on the table.

2   When a bird **lays** an egg, it pushes an egg out of its body.

lay

♥ Look at **lie**
Hello Kitty lay on the grass and looked at the sky.

layer *noun*
layers

A **layer** is something that covers a surface, or that lies between two other things.
A layer of new snow covered the street.

lazy *adjective*
lazier, laziest

A **lazy** person does not like working.
He was too lazy to read the whole book.

lead *verb*
leads, leading, led

If you **lead** someone to a place, you take them there.
Hello Kitty took her hand and started to lead her into the house.

lead *noun*

If you are in the **lead** in a race or competition, you are winning.
Our team was in the lead after ten minutes.

lead *noun*

Lead is a soft, grey, heavy metal.

leader *noun*
leaders

The **leader** of a group of people or a country is the person who is in charge of it.
Your team leaders have your instructions.

leaf *noun*
leaves

The **leaves** of a plant are the parts that are flat, thin, and usually green.
A dry, brown leaf floated on the water.

lean *verb*
leans, leaning, leant or **leaned**

When you **lean**, you bend your body from your waist.
Hello Kitty leant forwards and looked out the window.

leap *verb*
leaps, leaping, leapt or **leaped**

If you **leap**, you jump a long way or very high.
Hello Kitty leaped in the air and waved her hands.

learn *verb*
learns, learning, learnt or **learned**

When you **learn** something, you get to know it or how to do it.
When did you learn to swim?

leather *noun*

Leather is the skin of some animals that you can use for making things.
Is your jacket made of real leather?

leave *verb*
leaves, leaving, left

1   When you leave a place, you go away from it.
    Hello Kitty's bus leaves in an hour.

2   If you **leave** something somewhere, you do not bring it with you.
    Hello Kitty left her bags in the car.

leaves

💙 Look at **leaf**
The leaves are beginning to turn brown.

led

💙 Look at **lead**
The woman led me through the door into her office.

left *noun*

The **left** is one side of something. For example, on a page, English writing begins on the **left**.
Hello Kitty's school is on the left at the end of the road.

left

💙 Look at **leave**
Hello Kitty's teacher suddenly left the room.

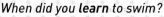

a
b
c
d
e
f
g
h
i
j
k
l
m
n
o
p
q
r
s
t
u
v
w
x
y
z

A
B
C
D
E
F
G
H
I
J
K
L
M
N
O
P
Q
R
S
T
U
V
W
X
Y
Z

leg *noun*
legs

1 A person's or animal's **legs** are the long parts of their body that they use for walking and standing.
Stand with your arms stretched out and your legs apart.

2 The **legs** of a table or chair are the long parts that it stands on.
One of the legs is loose.

lemon *noun*
lemons

A **lemon** is a yellow fruit with very sour juice.

lend *verb*
lends, lending, lent

If you **lend** someone something, you give it to them for a period of time and then they give it back to you.
Will you lend me your pen?

length *noun*
lengths

The **length** of something is how long it is from one end to the other.
The table is about a metre in length.

lent

 Look at **lend**
Hello Kitty lent her two books to read on holiday.

leopard *noun*
leopards

A **leopard** is a large, wild cat. **Leopards** have yellow fur with black spots, and live in Africa and Asia.

less *adjective*

Less means a smaller amount.
I am trying to spend less money on sweets.

lesson *noun*
lessons

A **lesson** is a period of time when someone teaches you something.
My sister has a piano lesson every Monday.

let *verb*
lets, letting, let

1 If you **let** someone do something, you allow them to do it.

2 You can say **let's** when you want someone to do something with you. **Let's** is short for **let us**.
Let's go!

letter *noun*
letters

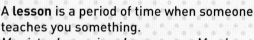

1 A **letter** is a message on paper that you post to someone.
Hello Kitty received a letter from a friend.

2 **Letters** are shapes that you write to make words.
Hello Kitty practised writing the letters in class.

lettuce *noun*
lettuces

A **lettuce** is a vegetable with large green leaves that you eat in salads.

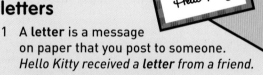

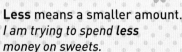

library *noun*
libraries

A **library** is a place where you can go to read or borrow books.
*Hello Kitty is going to the **library** to look for a book about whales.*

lick *verb*
licks, licking, licked

If you **lick** something, you move your tongue over it.
Lick the stamp before you put it on the envelope.

lid *noun*
lids

A **lid** is the top of a container that you can remove.
*Hello Kitty lifted the **lid** of the box.*

lie *verb*
lies, lying, lay, lain

When you **lie** somewhere, your body is flat, and you are not standing or sitting.
Lie on the bed and close your eyes for a while.

lie *noun*
lies

A **lie** is something you say that is not true.
*You told me a **lie**!*

life *noun*
lives

Your **life** is the period of time when you are alive.
*I want to live here for the rest of my **life**.*

lift *verb*
lifts, lifting, lifted

When you **lift** something, you take it and move it up.
*Hello Kitty **lifted** the bag on to her shoulder.*

light *noun*
lights

1 **Light** is the bright energy that comes from the sun, that lets you see things.
*A little **light** comes into the room through the thin curtains.*

2 A **light** is something like a lamp, that allows you to see.
*There was only one small **light** in the room.*

light *adjective*
lighter, lightest

1 If a place is **light**, it is bright because of the sun or lamps.
*It gets **light** at about 6 o'clock in the morning.*

2 Something that is **light** is not heavy.
*The chair is quite **light** so we can move it if we want to.*

3 A **light** colour is pale.
*Hello Kitty's skirt is **light** blue.*

light *verb*
lights, lighting, lit

When you **light** a fire, it starts burning.
*We used a whole box of matches to **light** the fire.*

lightning *noun*

Lightning is the very bright flashes of light in the sky in a storm.
*There was thunder and **lightning** and big black clouds in the sky.*

like

1 If things or people are **like** each other, they are almost the same.
*Hello Kitty and Mimmy are **like** each other.*

2 You say what something or someone is **like** when you are talking about how they seem to you.
*"What was Hello Kitty's party **like**?"
—"Oh it was great!"*

a b c d e f g h i j k l m n o p q r s t u v w x y z

A B C D E F G H I J K L 🌸 M N O P Q R S T U V W X Y Z

line *noun*
lines

A **line** is a long, thin mark or shape.
Hello Kitty drew a line at the bottom of the page.

lion *noun*
lions

A **lion** is a large wild cat that lives in Africa. **Lions** have yellow fur, and male **lions** have long hair on their head and neck.

lip *noun*
lips

Your **lips** are the edges of your mouth.
He bit his lip.

liquid *noun*
liquids

A **liquid** is something that you can pour. Water and oil are **liquids**.
The bottle is full of clear liquid.

list *noun*
lists

A **list** is a set of names or other things that you write one below the other.
There are six names on the list.

listen *verb*
listens, listening, listened

If you **listen** to something, you hear it and give it your attention.
Hello Kitty is listening to music.

lit

💜 Look at **light**
He took a match and lit the candle.

litre *noun*
litres

A **litre** is used for measuring liquid.

litter *noun*

Litter is rubbish that people drop in the street.
Please don't drop any litter.

little *adjective*
littler, littlest

A person or thing that is **little** is small in size.
They live in a little house.

live *verb*
lives, living, lived

1 You **live** in the place where your home is.
Where do you live?

2 To **live** means to be alive.
We all need water to live.

lives

💜 Look at **life**
Their lives were changed.

lizard *noun*
lizards

A **lizard** is a small reptile with a long tail and rough skin.

load *verb*
loads, loading, loaded

If you **load** a vehicle, you put something on it.
We finished loading the bags on to the lorry.

loaf *noun*
loaves

A **loaf** is bread that you cut into slices.
He bought a loaf of bread and some cheese.

lock *verb*
locks, locking, locked

When you **lock** a door, you close it with a key.
*Are you sure you **locked** the front door?*

log *noun*
logs

A **log** is a thick piece of wood from a tree.
*Hello Kitty sat in front of a **log** fire.*

lolly *noun*
lollies

A **lolly** is a sweet or ice cream on a stick.

long *adjective*
longer, longest

1 Something that is **long** takes a lot of time.
*Hello Kitty thought the afternoon seemed very **long**.*

2 Something that is **long** measures a great distance from one end to the other.
*There is a **long** table in the middle of the kitchen.*

look *verb*
looks, looking, looked

1 When you **look** at something, you turn your eyes so that you can see it.
*Hello Kitty **looked** at the clock.*

2 You use **look** when you describe how a person seems.
*Hello Kitty **looked** excited.*

loose *adjective*
looser, loosest

1 Something that is **loose** moves when it should not.
*One of the table legs is **loose**.*

2 **Loose** clothes are rather large and are not tight.
*Wear **loose**, comfortable clothes when you do the exercises.*

lorry *noun*
lorries

A **lorry** is a large vehicle for moving things by road.

lose *verb*
loses, losing, lost

1 If you **lose** a game, you do not win it.
*Our team **lost** the match by one point.*

2 If you **lose** something, you do not know where it is.
*Hello Kitty has **lost** her ball.*

lost *adjective*

If you are **lost**, you do not know where you are.
*I suddenly knew that I was **lost**.*

lot or lots

A **lot** of something, or **lots** of something, is a large amount of it.
*Hello Kitty has **lots** of friends.*

loud *adjective*
louder, loudest

A **loud** noise is a very big sound.
*The music was very **loud**.*

a b c d e f g h i j k **l** m n o p q r s t u v w x y z

SODA FOUNTAIN

COTTON CANDY

79

love verb
loves, loving, loved

1 If you **love** someone, you care very much about them.

2 If you **love** something, you like it very much.
Hello Kitty loves dancing.

lovely adjective
lovelier, loveliest

A **lovely** thing or person is very beautiful or very nice.
Hello Kitty thinks her new teacher is lovely.

low adjective
lower, lowest

1 Something that is **low** is close to the ground.
There is a low fence around Hello Kitty's house.

2 A **low** number is a small number.
The price was very low.

lucky adjective
luckier, luckiest

Someone who is **lucky** enjoys good things that people don't expect to happen.
He was lucky to win the competition.

lump noun
lumps

A **lump** is a solid piece of something.
There was a bowl full of lumps of sugar.

lunch noun
lunches

Lunch is the meal that you have in the middle of the day.

lying

♥ Look at **lie**
There was a dog lying on the ground.

Mm

machine noun
machines

A **machine** is a piece of equipment that uses electricity or an engine to do something.
My friend left a message on the answering machine.

made

♥ Look at **make**
Mum made me a big birthday cake.

magazine noun
magazines

A **magazine** is a thin book with stories and pictures in it.
Hello Kitty gets her favourite magazine every Thursday.

magic noun

In stories, **magic** is a special power that allows you to do impossible things.
By magic, the man turned to stone.

magnet noun
magnets

A **magnet** is a piece of metal that attracts iron towards it.

main adjective

The **main** thing is the most important one.
That's the main reason I want it.

make - mask

make *verb*
makes, making, made

1 If you **make** something, you put it together or build it from other things.
   *She **makes** all her own clothes.*

2 You can use **make** to show that a person does or says something.
   *He **made** a phone call.*

3 If you **make** a person do something, they must do it.
   *Mum **made** Hello Kitty tidy her bedroom.*

male *adjective*

A **male** person or animal could become a father.
*All of the puppies were **male**.*

mammal *noun*
mammals

Mammals are animals that feed their babies with milk.
*Some **mammals**, like dolphins, live in the sea.*

man *noun*
men

A **man** is an adult male person.
*The book is for both **men** and women.*

manage *verb*
manages, managing, managed

If you **manage** something, you control it.
*He **managed** the bank for 20 years.*

many *adjective*

If there are **many** people or things, there are a lot of them.
*Does he have **many** friends?*

map *noun*
maps

A **map** is a drawing of an area such as a city, country, or continent, showing its main features as if you looked at them from above.
*We studied a **map** of Africa in class today.*

March *noun*

March is the month after February and before April. It has 31 days.

mark *noun*
marks

1 A **mark** is a small dirty area on a surface.
   *I can't get this **mark** off my shirt.*

2 A **mark** is a shape that you write or draw.
   *Hello Kitty made a few **marks** with her pen.*

market *noun*
markets

A **market** is a place where people buy and sell things.
*There's a **market** in the town centre every Saturday morning.*

marmalade *noun*

Marmalade is jam that is made from oranges.

marry *verb*
marries, marrying, married

When a man and a woman **marry**, they become husband and wife.

mask *noun*
masks

A **mask** is something that you wear over your face to protect or hide it.

a b c d e f g h i j k l **m** n o p q r s t u v w x y z

mat *noun*
mats

A **mat** is a small piece of cloth, wood, or plastic that you put on a table to protect it.
Hello Kitty put her glass on a red mat.

match *noun*
matches

1 A **match** is a small, thin stick that makes a flame when you rub it on a rough surface.
She lit a match and held it up to the candle.

2 A **match** is a game of football, cricket, or some other sport.
We won all our matches last year.

match *verb*
matches, matching, matched

If one thing **matches** another, they look good together.
Do these shoes match my dress?

material *noun*
materials

1 **Material** is cloth.
Hello Kitty's skirt was made from pink and white material.

2 A **material** is what something is made of, like rock, glass or plastic.
Wax is a soft material.

maths *noun*

If you learn **maths**, you learn about numbers, shapes, and amounts.

matter *verb*
matters, mattered

If something **matters** to you, it is important.
Never mind, it doesn't matter.

may *verb*

1 If you **may** do something, it is possible that you will do it.
I may come back next year.

2 If you **may** do something, you can do it because someone allows you to do it.
Please may I leave the room?

May *noun*

May is the month after April and before June. It has 31 days.

me

You use **me** when you are talking about yourself.
Can you hear me?

meal *noun*
meals

A **meal** is food that you eat at one time. Breakfast, lunch and dinner are **meals**.
Hello Kitty sat next to me for every meal.

mean *verb*
means, meaning, meant

1 If you ask what something **means**, you want to understand it.
What does this word mean?

2 If you **mean** what you are saying, it is not a joke.
He says he loves her, and I think he means it.

3 If you mean to do something, it is not an accident.
I didn't mean to drop the cup.

A B C D E F G H I J K L M N O P Q R S T U V W X Y Z

mean *adjective*
meaner, meanest

Someone who is **mean** is not nice to other people.
He was sorry for being mean to her.

measles *noun*

Measles is an illness that gives you a fever and red spots on your skin.

measure *verb*
measures, measuring, measured

If you **measure** something, you find its size.
First measure the length of the table.

meat *noun*

Meat is the part of an animal that people cook and eat.
I don't eat meat or fish.

medicine *noun*

Medicine is something that you swallow to make you better when you are ill.
The medicine saved his life.

meet *verb*
meets, meeting, met

If you **meet** someone, you see them and you talk to them.
Hello Kitty met her friends in the park today.

melon *noun*
melons

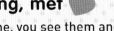

A **melon** is a large, soft, sweet fruit with a hard green or yellow skin.
Dad ate a big slice of melon.

melt *verb*
melts, melting, melted

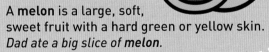

When something **melts**, it changes from a solid to a liquid as it becomes warmer.
Melt the chocolate in a bowl.

memory *noun*
memories

1 Your **memory** is the part of your mind that remembers things.
He has a very good memory for numbers.

2 A **memory** is something you remember about the past.
They discussed their memories of their school days.

men

💜 Look at **man**
He ordered his men to stop.

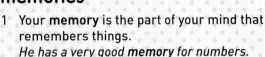

mend *verb*
mends, mending, mended

If you **mend** something that is broken, you repair it.
She mended the hole in his sock.

mess *noun*

If something is a **mess**, it is not neat.
After the party, the house was a mess.

message *noun*
messages

A **message** is a piece of information that you send someone.
Hello Kitty got emails and messages from friends on her birthday.

messy *adjective*
messier, messiest

A person or thing that is **messy** is not neat.
His writing is rather messy.

met

💜 Look at **meet**
Hello Kitty met her when she was on holiday.

a b c d e f g h i j k l **m** n o p q r s t u v w x y z

83

metal *noun*
metals

Metal is a hard material that melts when it gets very hot.
Gold, iron and lead are different kinds of metal.

metre *noun*
metres

A **metre** is used for measuring distances or how long things are.
The hole in the ground is about one and a half metres across.

mice

Look at **mouse**
You can hear the mice under the floor.

midday *noun*

Midday is twelve o'clock in the middle of the day.
At midday Hello Kitty played a game.

middle *noun*
middles

The **middle** of something is the part that is the same distance from each edge or end.
Hello Kitty stood in the middle of the room.

midnight *noun*

Midnight is twelve o'clock at night.
They went to bed after midnight.

might *verb*

You use **might** when something is possible.
Hello Kitty might come out to play later.

mile *noun*
miles

A **mile** is used for measuring distance.
They drove 600 miles across the desert.

milk *noun*

Milk is the white liquid that all baby mammals get from their mothers. People also drink **milk** that farmers get from cows.
They make cheese from goat's and sheep's milk too.

millilitre *noun*
millilitres

A **millilitre** is used for measuring liquid. There are 1000 **millilitres** in a litre.
I gave him the medicine with a 5 millilitre spoon.

millimetre *noun*
millimetres

A **millimetre** is used for measuring how long things are. There are 1000 **millimetres** in a metre.
The small insect was a few millimetres long.

mind *noun*
minds

Your **mind** is the part of your brain that thinks, understands and remembers.
I can't get that song out of my mind.

mind *verb*
minds, minding, minded

If you **mind** something, it annoys you.
It was hard work but Hello Kitty didn't mind.

mine

Mine means belonging to me.
That isn't your bag, it's mine.

mine *noun*
mines

A **mine** is a deep hole or tunnel where people go to dig things like gold or diamonds out of rock.

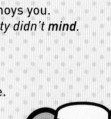

minus

You use **minus** when you take one number away from another number.
*Three **minus** two is one.*

minute *noun*
minutes

A **minute** is used for measuring time. There are sixty seconds in one **minute**.
*The food will take 20 **minutes** to cook.*

minute *adjective*

Something that is **minute** is very small.
*You only need to use a **minute** amount of glue.*

miss *verb*
misses, missing, missed

1 If you **miss** something that you are trying to hit or catch, you do not manage to hit it or catch it.
   *Hello Kitty jumped, but **missed** the ball.*

2 If you **miss** something, you do not notice it.
   *What did you say? Hello Kitty **missed** it.*

3 If you **miss** someone who is not with you, you feel sad that they are not there.
   *The boys **miss** their father.*

Miss

You use **Miss** in front of the name of a girl or a woman who is not married when you are talking to her or talking about her.
*Do you know **Miss** Smith?*

mistake *noun*
mistakes

A **mistake** is something that is not correct.
*I made three **mistakes** in my letter.*

mix *verb*
mixes, mixing, mixed

If you **mix** things, you put different things together to make something new.
***Mix** the sugar with the butter.*

mixture *noun*
mixtures

A **mixture** is what you make when you mix different things together.
*The drink is a **mixture** of orange and apple juice.*

mobile phone *noun*
mobile phones

A **mobile phone** is a small phone that you can take everywhere with you.

model *noun*
models

1 A **model** is a small copy of something.
   *Hello Kitty made the **model** house with paper and glue.*

2 A **model** is a person whose job is to wear and show new clothes.
   *The **model** in the picture was very tall.*

mole *noun*
moles

1 A **mole** is a natural dark spot on your skin.
   *She has a **mole** on the side of her nose.*

2 A **mole** is a small animal with black fur that lives under the ground.

moment *noun*
moments

A **moment** is a very short period of time.
*Hello Kitty stopped for a **moment**.*

Monday *noun*
Mondays

Monday is the day after Sunday and before Tuesday.
*Hello Kitty went back to school on **Monday**.*

money *noun*

Money is what you use to buy things.
*Cars cost a lot of **money**.*

monkey *noun*
monkeys

A **monkey** is an animal that has a long tail and can climb trees.

monster *noun*
monsters

In stories, a **monster** is a big, ugly creature that frightens people.
*The film is about a **monster** in the wardrobe.*

month *noun*
months

A **month** is one part of a year. There are twelve **months** in one year.
*Hello Kitty is going on holiday next **month**.*

moon *noun*
moons

The **moon** shines in the sky at night and moves around the earth every month.
*The first man on the **moon** was Neil Armstrong.*

more

You use **more** to talk about a greater amount of something.
*He has **more** chips than me.*

morning *noun*
mornings

The **morning** is the early part of the day, before lunch.
*What do you want to do tomorrow **morning**?*

most

1 **Most** of a group of things or people means nearly all of them.
   ***Most** of the houses here are very old.*

2 The **most** means the largest amount.
   *Who has the **most** money?*

moth *noun*
moths

A **moth** is an insect like a butterfly that usually flies at night.

A B C D E F G H I J K L M❀ N O P Q R S T U V W X Y Z

mother *noun*
mothers

A **mother** is a woman who has a child.

motorbike *noun*
motorbikes

A **motorbike** is a large bike with an engine.

motorway *noun*
motorways

A **motorway** is a wide road for travelling long distances fast.

mountain *noun*
mountains

A **mountain** is a very high area of land with steep sides.
*Ben Nevis is the highest **mountain** in Scotland.*

mouse *noun*
mice

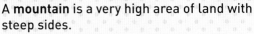

1 A **mouse** is a small animal with a long tail.
2 You use a **mouse** to move things on a computer screen.

mouth *noun*
mouths

Your **mouth** is the part of your face that you use for eating or talking.
*When you cough, please cover your **mouth**.*

move *verb*
moves, moving, moved

1 When you **move** something, you put it in a different place.
*The man asked her to **move** her car.*
2 If you **move**, you go to live in a different place.
*She's **moving** to London next month.*

Mr

You use **Mr** before a man's name when you are talking to him or talking about him.
*Our history teacher's name is **Mr** Jones.*

Mrs

You use **Mrs** before a married woman's name when you are talking to her or talking about her.
*How are you, **Mrs** Smith?*

Ms

You use **Ms** before a woman's name when you are talking to her or talking about her.
*The message is for **Ms** Clark.*

much

You use **much** to talk about a large amount of something.
*I ate too **much** food.*

mud *noun*

Mud is a mixture of earth and water.
*There was **mud** on Hello Kitty's shoes.*

muddy *adjective*
muddier, muddiest

If something is **muddy**, it is covered with mud.
*Hello Kitty's boots are all **muddy**.*

mug *noun*
mugs

A **mug** is a deep cup with straight sides.
*He poured tea into the **mugs**.*

a b c d e f g h i j k l **m** n o p q r s t u v w x y z

multiplication - myth

A B C D E F G H I J K L M N O P Q R S T U V W X Y Z

multiplication *noun*

Multiplication is when you multiply one number by another.

multiply *verb*
multiplies, multiplying, multiplied

If you **multiply** a number, you add it to itself a number of times.
*You get 24 if you **multiply** three by eight.*

mum or mummy *noun*
mums or **mummies**

Mum or **mummy** is a name for your mother.

muscle *noun*
muscles

Your **muscles** are the parts inside your body that help you move.
*Sport helps to keep your **muscles** strong.*

museum *noun*
museums

A **museum** is a building where you can look at interesting, old, and valuable things.
*Hello Kitty went to the **museum** to see the dinosaur bones.*

mushroom *noun*
mushrooms

A **mushroom** is a plant with a short stem and a round top that you can eat.
*There are many types of wild **mushroom**, and some of them are poisonous.*

music *noun*

Music is the sound that you make when you sing or play instruments. *What's your favourite **music**?*

musical instrument
noun
musical instruments

A **musical instrument** is an instrument that you use to play music, like a piano or a guitar.

must *verb*

You use **must** to show that you think something is very important.
*You **must** tell the police all the facts.*

mustn't

Mustn't is short for **must not**.
*I **mustn't** forget to take my key with me.*

my

You use **my** to show that something belongs to you.
*I went to sleep in **my** room.*

myself

You use **myself** when the you are talking about yourself.
*I hurt **myself** when I fell down.*

mystery *noun*
mysteries

A mystery is something that you do not understand or know about.
*Why she's crying is a **mystery**.*

myth *noun*
myths

A **myth** is a very old story about magic, and strange people and creatures.

88

Nn

nature *noun*

Nature is all the animals, plants, and other things in the world that people did not make or change.
*We watched **nature** all around us from our camp in the forest.*

nail *noun*
nails

1   A **nail** is a thin piece of metal. It is flat at one end and it has a point at the other end.
*A picture hung on a **nail** in the wall.*

2   Your **nails** are the thin hard parts that grow at the ends of your fingers and toes.
*Try to keep your **nails** short.*

naughty *adjective*
naughtier, naughtiest

A **naughty** child does things which are bad.
*She was so **naughty**, her mother sent her to bed early.*

near *adjective*
nearer, nearest

If something is **near** a place, thing, or person, it is not far away from them.
*We are very **near** Hello Kitty's house.*

name *noun*
names

A person's **name** is the word or words that you use to talk to them, or to talk about them.
*Is your **name** Hello Kitty?*

nearly

Nearly means almost.
*It's **nearly** five o'clock.*

neat *adjective*
neater, neatest

A **neat** place or person is clean and tidy.
*Hello Kitty made sure that her room was **neat** before she left.*

narrow *adjective*
narrower, narrowest

Something that is **narrow** is a small distance from one side to the other.
*Hello Kitty walked through the town's **narrow** streets.*

neck *noun*
necks

Your **neck** is the part of your body between your head and the rest of your body.
*Hello Kitty wore a gold chain around her **neck**.*

nasty *adjective*
nastier, nastiest

Something that is **nasty** is horrible.
*That's a **nasty** thing to say!*

natural *adjective*

Natural things come from nature.
*The **natural** home of these animals is under the ground.*

necklace *noun*
necklaces

A **necklace** is a chain of beads or jewels that you wear around your neck.
*Hello Kitty is wearing a beautiful **necklace**.*

need *verb*
needs, needing, needed

If you **need** something, you believe that you must have it or do it.
I need some more money.

needle *noun*
needles

A **needle** is a small, thin metal tool with a sharp point that you use for sewing.
If you get me a needle and thread, I'll sew the button on.

needn't

Needn't is short for **need not**.
You needn't come with us if you don't want to.

neighbour *noun*
neighbours

Your **neighbours** are the people who live around you.
Hello Kitty met her neighbour when she went to the shops.

nephew *noun*
nephews

Someone's **nephew** is the son of their sister or brother.
I have a nephew who is still a baby.

nervous *adjective*

If you are **nervous** about something, it worries you and you are rather afraid.
I tried not to show that I was nervous.

nest *noun*
nests

A **nest** is the place where a bird keeps its eggs or its babies.
There were six small eggs in the bird's nest.

net *noun*
nets

A **net** is made from pieces of string or rope tied together with holes between them. It is for catching things like fish, or the ball in some sports.
The idea is to throw the ball into the top of the net.

never

Never means at no time in the past, present or future.
Never look straight at the sun.

new *adjective*
newer, newest

1   Something that is **new** was not there before.
    They discovered a new medicine for his illness.

2   If something is **new**, nobody has used it before.
    Hello Kitty is wearing her new shoes.

3   A **new** thing or person is a different one from the one you had before.
    Hello Kitty has a new teacher.

news *noun*

News is information that you did not know before.
We waited and waited for news of him.

newspaper *noun*
newspapers

A **newspaper** is a number of large sheets of paper with news and other information printed on them.
They read about it in the newspaper.

next *adjective*

The **next** thing is the one that comes immediately after this one or after the last one.
Hello Kitty got up early the next morning.

nice *adjective*
nicer, nicest

If something is **nice**, you like it.
*Hello Kitty lives in a really **nice** house.*

niece *noun*
nieces

Someone's **niece** is the daughter of their sister or brother.
*He bought a present for his **niece**.*

night *noun*
nights

The **night** is the time when it is dark outside, and most people sleep.
*It's eleven o'clock at **night** in Beijing.*

nightdress *noun*
nightdresses

A **nightdress** is a loose dress that a woman or girl can wear to sleep in.

nightmare *noun*
nightmares

A **nightmare** is a dream that frightens or worries you.
*She had a **nightmare** last night.*

nine *noun*

Nine is the number **9**.

no

You use **no** to say that something is not true or to refuse something.
*"Would you like a drink?"—"**No** thank you."*

nobody *noun*

Nobody means not one person.
*For a long time, **nobody** spoke.*

nod *verb*
nods, nodding, nodded

When you **nod**, you move your head up and down, usually to show that you agree.
*Hello Kitty **nodded** when I asked if she wanted to come.*

noise *noun*
noises

A **noise** is a loud sound.
*She made a loud banging **noise** with her hammer.*

noisy *adjective*
noisier, noisiest

A **noisy** person or thing makes a lot of loud noise.
*It was a very **noisy** party.*

none

None means not one or not any.
***None** of us knew her.*

nonsense *noun*

If something is **nonsense**, it is not true or it is silly.
*My father said the story was **nonsense**.*

noon *noun*

Noon is twelve o'clock in the middle of the day.
*The lesson started at **noon**.*

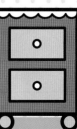

a b c d e f g h i j k l m **n** o p q r s t u v w x y z

A B C D E F G H I J K L M **N** O P Q R S T U V W X Y Z

north *noun*

The **north** is the direction to your left when you are looking towards the place where the sun rises.

nose *noun*
noses

Your **nose** is the part of your face above your mouth that you use for breathing and for noticing smells.
Hello Kitty points to her nose.

nostril *noun*
nostrils

Your **nostrils** are the two holes at the end of your nose.
Keeping your mouth closed, breathe in through your nostrils.

note *noun*
notes

1   A **note** is a short letter or message.
Hello Kitty wrote her a note and left it on the table.

2   A **note** is one musical sound.
Hello Kitty played some notes on her recorder.

nothing

Nothing means not anything.
There was nothing to do.

notice *verb*
notices, noticing, noticed

If you **notice** something, you suddenly see or hear it.
Did you notice Hello Kitty leave the room?

notice *noun*
notices

A **notice** is a sign that gives information or instructions.
The notice said "Please close the door."

noun *noun*
nouns

A **noun** is a word that is used for talking about a person or thing. Examples of **nouns** are "child", "table", "sun", and "strength".

November *noun*

November is the month after October and before December. It has 30 days.

now

You use **now** to talk about the present time.
Hello Kitty has to leave now.

nowhere

Nowhere means not anywhere.
There's nowhere quiet for Hello Kitty to do her homework.

number *noun*
numbers

A **number** is a word that you use to count.
What number is your house?

nurse *noun*
nurses

A **nurse** is a person whose job is to care for people who are ill.
She thanked the nurses at the hospital.

nut *noun*
nuts

A **nut** is a dry fruit with a hard shell.
Nuts and seeds are very good for you.

Oo

oak noun
oaks

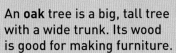

An **oak** tree is a big, tall tree with a wide trunk. Its wood is good for making furniture.

oar noun
oars

An **oar** is a long piece of wood with a wide, flat end, used for moving a boat through the water.

obey verb
obeys, obeying, obeyed

If you **obey** a person or an order, you do what you are told to do.

ocean noun
oceans

An **ocean** is a big sea.
We crossed the Atlantic Ocean.

o'clock noun

You say **o'clock** when saying what time it is.
It is eight o'clock in the morning.

octagon noun
octagons

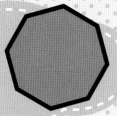

An **octagon** is a shape with eight straight sides.

October noun

October is the month after September and before November. It has 31 days.

octopus noun
octopuses

An **octopus** is a soft ocean animal with eight long arms.

odd adjective
odder, oddest

1   If something is **odd**, it is strange or unusual.
    There was an odd smell in the kitchen.

2   You say that two things are **odd** when they do not belong to the same set or pair.
    Hello Kitty is wearing odd socks.

3   **Odd** numbers, such as 3 and 17, are numbers that cannot be divided by the number two.

off

1   If you take something **off** another thing, it is no longer on it.
    Hello Kitty took her book off the desk.

2   When something that uses electricity is **off**, it is not using electricity.
    The light was off.

offer verb
offers, offering, offered

If you **offer** something to someone, you ask them if they would like to have it.
The man offered his seat to Hello Kitty.

office noun
offices

An **office** is a room where people work at desks.

often

Something that happens **often** happens many times or a lot of the time.

oil noun

Oil is a thick liquid.
We need some cooking oil.

old *adjective*
older, oldest

1 An **old** person is someone who has lived for a long time.
An old lady sat next to me.

2 An **old** thing is something that somebody made a long time ago.
We have a very old car.

on

1 If someone or something is **on** a surface, it is resting there.
There was a large box on the table.

2 When something that uses electricity is **on**, it is using electricity.
The television is on.

once

If something happens **once**, it happens one time only.
Hello Kitty met her once, at a party.

one *noun*

One is the number **1**.

onion *noun*
onions

An **onion** is a small, round vegetable with a brown skin like paper and a very strong taste.

only

1 If you talk about the **only** thing or person, you mean that there are no others.
It was the only shop in the town.

2 You use **only** when you are saying how small or short something is.
Hello Kitty's house is only a few miles from here.

3 If you are an **only** child, you have no brothers or sisters.

open *verb*
opens, opening, opened

1 When you **open** something, or when it **opens**, you move it so that it is no longer closed.
Hello Kitty opened the door.

2 When a shop or office **opens**, people are able to go in.
The banks will open again on Monday morning.

opposite

1 If one thing is **opposite** another, it is across from it.
Hello Kitty sat opposite Mummy at breakfast.

2 If things are **opposite**, they are as different as they can be.
Hello Kitty watched the cars driving in the opposite direction.

orange *noun*

1 An **orange** is a round fruit with a thick skin and lots of juice.

2 **Orange** is a colour between red and yellow.
Tigers are orange with black stripes.

orchestra *noun*
orchestras

An **orchestra** is a large group of people who play music together.
The orchestra began to play.

order *verb*
orders, ordering, ordered

If you **order** someone to do something, you tell them to do it.
She ordered him to leave.

ordinary *adjective*

Ordinary means not special or different in any way.
It was just an ordinary day.

other *adjective*
others

Other people or things are different people or things.
All the other children had gone home.

our

You use **our** to show that something belongs to you and one or more other people.
Our house is near the school.

ours

You use **ours** when you are talking about something that belongs to you and one or more other people.
That car is ours.

out

1 If you go **out** of a place, you leave it.
Hello Kitty ran out of the house.

2 If you are **out**, you are not at home.
I called Hello Kitty yesterday, but she was out.

3 If a light is **out**, it is no longer shining.
All the lights were out in Hello Kitty's house.

outside

1 The **outside** of something is the part that covers the rest of it.
They are painting the outside of the building.

2 If you are **outside**, you are not in a building.
Let's play outside.

oval *adjective*

Oval things have a shape like an egg.
She has an oval table.

oven *noun*
ovens

An **oven** is the part of a cooker like a large metal box with a door.

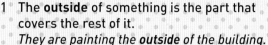

over

1 If one thing is **over** another thing, the first thing is above or higher than the second thing.
There was a lamp over the table.

2 If something is **over**, it has finished.
The class is over.

owe *verb*
owes, owing, owed

If you **owe** money to someone, you have to pay money to them.
He owes me £5.

owl *noun*
owls

An **owl** is a bird with large eyes that hunts at night.

own

You use **own** to say that something belongs to you.
Hello Kitty wanted her own room.

ox *noun*
oxen

An **ox** is a kind of bull that is used for carrying or pulling things.

Pp

pack verb
packs, packing, packed
When you **pack** a bag, you put clothes and other things into it, because you are going away.

paddle noun
paddles
A **paddle** is a short oar. You use it to move a small boat through water.

paddle verb
paddles, paddling, paddled
1   If someone **paddles** a boat, they move it using a paddle.
2   If you **paddle**, you walk in shallow water.

page noun
pages
A **page** is one side of a piece of paper in a book, a magazine, or a newspaper.
Turn to page 4.

paid
♥ Look at **pay**
Daddy paid for Hello Kitty's sweets.

pain noun
pains
Pain is the feeling that you have in a part of your body, because of illness or an accident.
I felt a sudden sharp pain in my ankle.

painful adjective
If a part of your body is **painful**, it hurts.
His right knee is very painful.

paint noun
paints
Paint is a liquid used to decorate buildings, or to make a picture.
Can I use some of your red paint?

paint verb
paints, painting, painted
1   If you **paint** something on a piece of paper or cloth, you make a picture of it using **paint**.
Hello Kitty likes painting flowers.
2   If you **paint** a wall or a door, you cover it with **paint**.

painting noun
paintings
A **painting** is a picture made with paint.
Hello Kitty is doing a painting of a bowl of fruit.

pair noun
pairs
A **pair** of things is two things of the same size and shape that are used together.
Hello Kitty wore a pair of black shoes.

palace *noun*
palaces

A **palace** is a very large house where important people live.

pale *adjective*
paler, palest

A **pale** colour is not strong or bright.
*Hello Kitty is wearing a **pale** blue dress.*

palm *noun*
palms

1   A **palm** or a **palm tree** is a tree that grows in hot countries. It has long leaves at the top, and no branches.

2   The **palm** of your hand is the inside part of your hand, between your fingers and your wrist.

panda *noun*
pandas

A **panda** is a large animal with black and white fur.

pantomime *noun*
pantomimes

A **pantomime** is a play that has a funny story with music and songs.

paper *noun*
papers

1   **Paper** is a material that you write on or wrap things with.
*Hello Kitty wrote her name on a piece of **paper**.*

2   A **paper** is a newspaper.

parcel *noun*
parcels

A **parcel** is something that is wrapped in paper.

parent *noun*
parents

Your **parents** are your mother and father.

park *noun*
parks

A **park** is a place with grass and trees. People go to **parks** to take exercise or play games.

park *verb*
parks, parking, parked

When someone **parks** a car, they leave it somewhere.
*They **parked** in the street outside the house.*

parrot *noun*
parrots

A **parrot** is a bird with a curved beak and bright feathers.
Parrots' feet have two toes at the front and two at the back.

part *noun*
parts

Part of something is a piece of it.

party *noun*
parties

A **party** is a time when people meet to have fun.
*Hello Kitty is having a birthday **party**.*

pass *verb*
passes, passing, passed

1   When you **pass** someone, you go by them.
*We **passed** them on our way here.*

2   If you **pass** something to someone, you give it to them.
*Hello Kitty **passed** a note to her friend.*

3   If you **pass** a test, you do well.

passenger *noun*
passengers

A **passenger** is a person who is travelling in a vehicle, but who is not driving.

A B C D E F G H I J K L M N O P Q R S T U V W X Y Z

past *noun*

The **past** is the period of time before now.
*In the **past**, there weren't any computers.*

past

1 Something that is **past** a place
   is on the other side of it.
   *It's just **past** the school there.*

2 You use **past** when you are telling the time.
   *It was ten **past** eleven.*

pasta *noun*

Pasta is a mixture of flour, eggs, and water.
Pasta comes in lots of shapes, even letters of the alphabet.

paste *verb*
pastes, pasting, pasted

1 If you **paste** something on to a surface, you
   stick it with glue.

2 If you **paste** words or pictures on a computer,
   you copy them from one place and put them
   somewhere new.
   *You can **paste** by holding down the Ctrl key and
   pressing V.*

pastry *noun*

Pastry is a mixture of flour,
butter, and water. People make it
flat and thin so that they can use it to make pies.

path *noun*
paths

A **path** is a strip of ground that people walk along.
*Hello Kitty followed the **path** along the cliff.*

patient *adjective*

If you are **patient**, you don't get angry quickly.

patient *noun*
patients

A **patient** is someone that a nurse or a doctor is
looking after.

pattern *noun*
patterns

A **pattern** is a group
of repeated shapes.
*Hello Kitty had a striped
pattern on her dress.*

paw *noun*
paws

The **paws** of an animal such
as a cat, dog, or bear are its feet.
*The puppy has four white **paws**.*

pay *verb*
pays, paying, paid

If you **pay** for something, you give someone an
amount of money for it.
*Did you **pay** for those sweets?*

peach *noun*
peaches

A **peach** is a round fruit with
a soft red and orange skin.

peanut *noun*
peanuts

Peanuts are small nuts that you can eat.

pear *noun*
pears

A **pear** is a fruit which is narrow
at the top and wide and round at the bottom.

peas *noun*

Peas are small, round, green vegetables.

pebble *noun*
pebbles

A **pebble** is a small, smooth stone.

pedal *noun*
pedals

The **pedals** on a bicycle are the two parts that you push with your feet to make the bicycle move.

peel *noun*

The **peel** of a fruit is its skin.

peg *noun*
pegs

A **peg** is a small piece of metal or wood on a wall that you hang things on.

pen *noun*
pens

A **pen** is a long thin tool that you use for writing with ink.

pencil *noun*
pencils

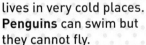

A **pencil** is a thin piece of wood with a black material through the middle that you use to write or draw with.

penguin *noun*
penguins

A **penguin** is a black and white bird that lives in very cold places. **Penguins** can swim but they cannot fly.

pentagon *noun*
pentagons

A **pentagon** is a shape with five straight sides.

people *noun*

People are men, women, and children. *Lots of **people** came to Hello Kitty's party.*

pepper *noun*
peppers

1 **Pepper** is a powder with a hot taste that you put on food.
2 A **pepper** is a green, red or yellow vegetable with seeds inside it.

period *noun*
periods

A **period** is a length of time.

person *noun*
people

A **person** is a man, a woman, or a child.

pest *noun*
pests

Pests are insects or small animals that damage crops or food.

pet *noun*
pets

A **pet** is a tame animal that you keep in your home.

A B C D E F G H I J K L M N O P 🌸 Q R S T U V W X Y Z

petal *noun*
petals

The **petals** of a flower are the thin parts on the outside that are a bright colour.

phone *noun*
phones

A **phone** is a piece of equipment that you use to talk to someone in another place.
*Two minutes later the **phone** rang.*

photograph *noun*
photographs

A **photograph** is a picture that you take with a camera.
*Hello Kitty took lots of **photographs** of her friends.*

piano *noun*
pianos

A **piano** is a large instrument for playing music. You play it by pressing the black and white keys.

pick *verb*
picks, picking, picked

1 If you **pick** someone, you choose them.
2 When you **pick** flowers, fruit, or leaves, you take them from a plant or tree.
   *Hello Kitty has **picked** some flowers from the garden.*

picnic *noun*
picnics

When people have a **picnic**, they eat a meal outside, usually in a park or a forest, or at the beach.
*Hello Kitty is going on a **picnic** tomorrow.*

picture *noun*
pictures

A **picture** is a drawing or painting.

pie *noun*
pies

A **pie** is a dish of fruit, meat, or vegetables that is covered with pastry and baked.
*Hello Kitty gave me a slice of apple **pie**.*

piece *noun*
pieces

A **piece** of something is a part of it.
*You must only take one **piece** of cake.*

pig *noun*
pigs

A **pig** is a farm animal with a fat body and short legs.

pigeon *noun*
pigeons

A **pigeon** is a large grey bird.

pile *noun*
piles

A **pile** of things is several of them lying on top of each other.
*Hello Kitty searched through the **pile** of boxes.*

pill *noun*
pills

Pills are small solid round pieces of medicine that you swallow.

pillow *noun*
pillows

A **pillow** is something soft that you rest your head on when you are in bed.

pilot *noun*
pilots

A **pilot** is a person who controls an aircraft.

pin *noun*
pins

A **pin** is a very small thin piece of metal with a point at one end.

pineapple *noun*
pineapples

A **pineapple** is a large sweet yellow fruit with a lot of juice. Its skin is brown, thick, and very rough.

pipe *noun*
pipes

A **pipe** is a long tube that water or gas can flow through.
They are going to take out the old water pipes.

pirate *noun*
pirates

Pirates are people who attack ships and steal things from them. *They have to find the pirates and the hidden gold.*

pizza *noun*
pizzas

A **pizza** is a flat, round piece of bread. **Pizzas** are covered with cheese and tomatoes. *Bake the pizza in a hot oven.*

place *noun*
places

1 A **place** is a building, area, town, or country. *This is the place where Hello Kitty was born.*

2 A **place** is also where something belongs. *Hello Kitty put the picture back in its place on the shelf.*

plain *adjective*
plainer, plainest

Something that is **plain** is ordinary and not special.

plan *noun*
plans

A **plan** is a way of doing something that you work out before you do it.
I've got a plan for getting out of here.

plane *noun*
planes

A **plane** is a large vehicle with wings and engines that flies through the air.

planet *noun*
planets

You find **planets** in space. They move around stars. The Earth is a **planet**.

a b c d e f g h i j k l m n o **p** q r s t u v w x y z

A B C D E F G H I J K L M N O P Q R S T U V W X Y Z

plant *noun*
plants

A **plant** is a living thing that grows in the earth. **Plants** have a stem, leaves, and roots.

plaster *noun*
plasters

1 A **plaster** is a strip of material with a soft part in the middle. You can cover a cut on your body with a **plaster**.

2 **Plaster** is a paste which people put on walls and ceilings so that they are smooth. *There were huge cracks in the **plaster**.*

plastic *noun*

Plastic is a material that is light but strong. It is made in factories. *Hello Kitty put her sweets in a **plastic** bag.*

plate *noun*
plates

A **plate** is a flat dish that is used for holding food. *Hello Kitty pushed her **plate** away.*

platform *noun*
platforms

A **platform** in a station is the place where you wait for a train.

play *verb*
plays, playing, played

1 When you **play**, you spend time using toys and taking part in games. *Hello Kitty was **playing** with her dolls.*

2 If you **play** an instrument, you make music with it.

playground *noun*
playgrounds

A **playground** is a special area where children can play.

please

You say **please** when you are asking someone to do something. *Can you help us, **please**?*

plenty *noun*

If there is **plenty** of something, there is a lot of it. *Don't worry. There's still **plenty** of time.*

plough *noun*
ploughs

A **plough** is a large tool that is used on a farm. Farmers pull it across a field to make the earth loose, so that they can plant seeds.

plus

You say **plus** to show that you are adding one number to another. *Two **plus** two is four.*

pocket *noun*
pockets

A **pocket** is a small bag that is part of your clothes. *Hello Kitty put the key in her **pocket**.*

poem *noun*
poems

A **poem** is a piece of writing. When people write a **poem**, they choose the words in a very careful way, so that they sound beautiful.

point *noun*
points

1 The **point** of something is its thin, sharp end. Needles and knives have **points**.

2 A **point** is a mark that you win in a game or a sport.

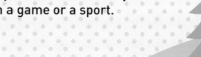

point *verb*
points, pointing, pointed

If you **point** at something, you stick out your finger to show where it is.
*Hello Kitty **pointed** at the boy sitting near her.*

poisonous *adjective*

Something that is **poisonous** will kill you or hurt you if you swallow or touch it.

polar bear *noun*
polar bears

A **polar bear** is a large white bear which lives in the area around the North Pole.

police *noun*

The **police** are the people who make sure that people obey the law.

polite *adjective*

Someone who is **polite** behaves well.

pond *noun*
ponds

A **pond** is a small area of water.
*Hello Kitty went to feed the ducks on the **pond**.*

pony *noun*
ponies

A **pony** is a small horse.

poor *adjective*
poorer, poorest

Someone who is **poor** doesn't have much money and doesn't own many things.

possible *adjective*

If something is **possible** it can happen.

post *verb*
posts, posting, posted

If you **post** a letter, you put a stamp on it and send it to someone.

poster *noun*
posters

A **poster** is a large notice or picture that you stick on a wall.

potato *noun*
potatoes

Potatoes are hard round white vegetables with brown or red skins. They grow under the ground.

a b c d e f g h i j k l m n o **p** q r s t u v w x y z

A B C D E F G H I J K L M N O P Q R S T U V W X Y Z

pour *verb*
pours, pouring, poured

If you **pour** something like water, you make it flow out of a container.

powder *noun*

Powder is a fine dry dust, like flour.

power *noun*

1   If someone has **power**, they have control over people.
    *He has the **power** to keep you in after school.*

2   The **power** of something is its strength.
    *The engine doesn't often work at full **power**.*

practise *verb*
practises, practising, practised

If you **practise** something, you do it often in order to do it better.
*Hello Kitty has been **practising** her sums.*

present *noun*
presents

1   The **present** is the period of time that is taking place now.

2   A **present** is something that you give to someone for them to keep.
    *He gave Hello Kitty a **present** for her birthday.*

present *adjective*

If someone is **present** somewhere, they are there.
*Hello Kitty wasn't **present** when they called out her name.*

press *verb*
presses, pressing, pressed

If you **press** something, you push it hard.
Press the blue button.

pretend *verb*
pretends, pretending, pretended

When you **pretend**, you act as if something is true, when you know it isn't.
*She **pretended** to be the teacher.*

pretty *adjective*
prettier, prettiest

If something is **pretty**, it is nice to look at.
*Hello Kitty has a **pretty** flower in her hair.*

price *noun*
prices

The **price** of something is how much you have to pay to buy it.
*Could you tell me the **price** of this car, please?*

prick *verb*
pricks, pricking, pricked

If you **prick** something, you stick something sharp like a pin or a knife into it.
*She **pricked** her finger on a pin.*

prince *noun*
princes

A **prince** is a boy or a man in the family of a king or queen.

princess noun
princesses

A **princess** is a girl or a woman in the family of a king or queen.

print verb
prints, printing, printed

1 If you **print** something, you use a machine to put words or pictures on paper.
2 If you **print** when you are writing, you do not join the letters together.

prison noun
prisons

A **prison** is a building where people who have broken the law are kept as a punishment.
He was sent to prison for five years.

prize noun
prizes

A **prize** is money or a special thing that you give to the person who wins a game, a race, or a competition.
Tippy won first prize.

problem noun
problems

A **problem** is something or someone that makes thing difficult, or that makes you worry.

program noun
programs

A **program** is a set of instructions that a computer uses to do a job.

programme noun
programmes

A **programme** is a television or radio show.
Hello Kitty is watching her favourite television programme.

project noun
projects

A **project** is a plan that takes a lot of time and effort.
It was a large building project.

promise verb
promises, promising, promised

If you **promise** to do something, you say that you will be sure to do it.
I promise that I'll help you all I can.

pronoun noun
pronouns

A **pronoun** is a word that you use in place of a noun when you are talking about someone or something. 'It' and 'she' are **pronouns**.

proper adjective

The **proper** thing or way is the one that is right.
Put things in their proper place.

protect verb
protects, protecting, protected

If you **protect** something, you keep it safe.
Make sure you protect your skin from the sun.

proud adjective
prouder, proudest

If you feel **proud**, you feel pleased about something good that you or other people close to you have done.
Hello Kitty was proud of her team today.

pudding noun
puddings

A **pudding** is something sweet that you eat after your main meal.
He ate a delicious chocolate pudding.

a b c d e f g h i j k l m n o **p** q r s t u v w x y z

A B C D E F G H I J K L M N O P Q R S T U V W X Y Z

puddle *noun*
puddles

A **puddle** is a small amount of water on the ground.
Splashing in puddles is lots of fun.

pull *verb*
pulls, pulling, pulled

When you **pull** something, you hold it and move it towards you.
The dentist had to pull out all his teeth.

punishment *noun*
punishments

Punishment is something done to someone because they have done something wrong.
His father sent him to bed early as a punishment for being rude.

pupil *noun*
pupils

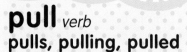

The **pupils** at a school are the children who go there.
Around 200 pupils go to Hello Kitty's school.

puppet *noun*
puppets

A **puppet** is a small model of a person or animal that you can move.

puppy *noun*
puppies

A **puppy** is a young dog.

purple *noun*

Purple is a mixture of red and blue.
Some grapes are purple.

purse *noun*
purses

A **purse** is a small bag that women use to carry money and other things.
Hello Kitty reached in her purse for her money.

push *verb*
pushes, pushing, pushed

When you **push** something, you press it in order to move it away from you.
Hello Kitty pushed back her chair and stood up.

put *verb*
puts, putting, put

When you **put** something somewhere, you move it there.
Hello Kitty put the book on the desk.

puzzle *verb*
puzzles, puzzling, puzzled

If something **puzzles** you, you do not understand it and you feel confused.
There was something about her that puzzled me.

pyjamas *noun*

Pyjamas are loose trousers and a jacket that you wear in bed.

pyramid *noun*
pyramids

A **pyramid** is a solid shape with a flat base and flat sides that make a point where they meet at the top.

Qq

quack *verb*
quacks, quacking, quacked

When a duck **quacks**, it makes a loud sound.
There were ducks quacking on the lawn.

quarrel *noun*
quarrels

A **quarrel** is an angry argument between people.
I had an awful quarrel with my brothers.

quarter *noun*
quarters

A **quarter** is one of four equal parts of something.
Hello Kitty counted a quarter of the class.

queen *noun*
queens

A **queen** is a woman who rules a country, or a woman who is married to a king.
Hello Kitty would love to meet the queen.

question *noun*
questions

A **question** is something that you say or write to ask a person about something.
Hello Kitty wrote her question on a piece of paper.

queue *noun*
queues

A **queue** is a line of people or cars waiting for something.
Hello Kitty stood in the bus queue for ten minutes.

quick *adjective*
quicker, quickest

Something that is **quick** moves or does things with great speed.
Daniel's car was very quick.

quickly

If you move or do something **quickly** you do it with great speed.
Hello Kitty ran quickly along the street.

quiet *adjective*
quieter, quietest

Someone who is **quiet** makes only a small amount of noise or no noise at all.
The baby was so quiet I didn't know he was there.

quite

Quite means a bit but not a lot.
I quite like her but she's not my best friend.

quiz *noun*
quizzes

A **quiz** is a game in which someone asks you questions to find out what you know.
After dinner we had a TV quiz and our team won.

a
b
c
d
e
f
g
h
i
j
k
l
m
n
o
p
q
r
s
t
u
v
w
x
y
z

Rr

rabbit *noun*
rabbits

A **rabbit** is a small animal with long ears.
Rabbits live in holes in the ground.
*My cousin has a pet **rabbit**.*

race *noun*
races

A **race** is a competition to see who is fastest,
for example in running or driving.
*Nobody can beat my sister in a **race**.*

radiator *noun*
radiators

A **radiator** is a metal thing filled with hot water
or steam. **Radiators** keep rooms warm.
*I burned myself on the **radiator** in the bathroom.*

radio *noun*
radios

A **radio** is a piece of equipment you use to hear
programmes with talking, news and music.
*Turn on the **radio** for the news please.*

railway *noun*
railways

A **railway** is a special road for trains, with
stations along it. **Railways** have two metal lines
that are always the same distance apart.
*The house was beside the **railway**.*

rain *noun*

Rain is water that falls from the clouds in drops.
*Hello Kitty's mother told her not to go out in the **rain**.*

rainbow *noun*
rainbows

A **rainbow** is
a half circle of
different colours in the sky.
You can sometimes see a **rainbow** when it rains.
*A **rainbow** appeared when the storm was over.*

ran

♥ Look at **run**
*Hello Kitty **ran** to school because she was late.*

rang

♥ Look at **ring**
*I got worried when the phone **rang**.*

rare *adjective*
rarer, rarest

Something that is **rare** is not seen or heard very
often.
*We are lucky to see this bird because it is very **rare**.*

raspberry *noun*
raspberries

A **raspberry** is a small soft red fruit. **Raspberries**
grow on bushes.
*Would you like some **raspberries** with your ice
cream?*

rat *noun*
rats

A **rat** is an animal that looks like a mouse.
A **rat** has a long tail and sharp teeth.
*The old house was full of **rats**.*

A B C D E F G H I J K L M N O P Q R S T U V W X Y Z

rather

You use **rather** to mean "a little bit".
*I thought the party was **rather** boring.*

raw *adjective*

Raw food has not been cooked.
*There is a bowl of **raw** carrots on the table.*

reach *verb*
reaches, reaching, reached

1   When you **reach** a place, you arrive there.
*We will not **reach** home until midnight.*

2   If you **reach** somewhere, you move your arm
and hand to take or touch something.
*Hello Kitty **reached** into her bag and brought
out a pen.*

read *verb*
reads, reading, read

When you **read**, you look at
written words and understand them,
and sometimes say them aloud.
*Her father **reads** Hello Kitty a
story every night before she goes to sleep.*

ready *adjective*

If you are **ready**, you are able to do something or
go somewhere right now.
*It takes Hello Kitty ages to get **ready** for school.*

real *adjective*

1   Something that is **real** is true and is not
imagined.
*No, it wasn't a dream. It was **real**.*

2   If something is **real**, it is not a copy.
*Is your necklace **real** gold?*

really

1   You say **really** to show how much you mean
something.
*Hello Kitty is **really** sorry she can't go to the party.*

2   You say **really** to show that what you are
saying is true.
*Are we **really** going to get a dog?*

reason *noun*
reasons

The **reason** for something is the fact which
explains why it happens.
*You must have a good **reason** for being so late.*

receive *verb*
receives, receiving, received

When you **receive** something, someone gives it
to you, or you get it after it has been sent to you.
*Did you **receive** the birthday card I sent you?*

recipe *noun*
recipes

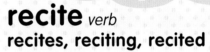

A **recipe** is a list of food
and a set of instructions
telling you how to cook something.
*Do you have a **recipe** for chocolate cake?*

recite *verb*
recites, reciting, recited

When someone **recites** a poem or other piece of
writing, they say it aloud after they have learned it.
*Hello Kitty listened to me **recite** the poem.*

record *noun*
records

A **record** is the best result ever.
*What's the world **record** for the 100 metres?*

record *verb*
records, recording, recorded

If you **record** something like a TV programme, you
make a copy of it so that you can watch it later.
*Can you **record** the football for me please?*

recorder *noun*
recorders

A **recorder** is a small instrument in the shape of
a pipe. You play a **recorder** by blowing into it and
putting your fingers over the holes in it.
*He has been learning the **recorder** for three years.*

a b c d e f g h i j k l m n o p q **r** s t u v w x y z

A B C D E F G H I J K L M N O P Q R S T U V W X Y Z

rectangle *noun*
rectangles

A **rectangle** is a shape with four straight sides.

red *noun*

Red is the colour of blood or a strawberry.
Hello Kitty's dress is bright red.

reflection *noun*
reflections

A **reflection** is something you can see on a smooth, shiny surface. What you see is really in a different place.
Reflections show things the wrong way round.

refuse *verb*
refuses, refusing, refused

If you **refuse** to do something, you say that you will not do it.
He refuses to have a bath.

remember *verb*
remembers, remembering, remembered

If you **remember** people or things from the past, you can bring them into your mind and think about them.
Hello Kitty remembers the first time she met him.

remind *verb*
reminds, reminding, reminded

If someone **reminds** you about something, they help you to remember it.
Remind me to buy a bottle of milk, will you?

remove *verb*
removes, removing, removed

If you **remove** something from a place, you take it away.
When the cake is cooked, remove it from the oven.

repair *verb*
repairs, repairing, repaired

If you **repair** something that is damaged or broken, you fix it so that it works again.
The man managed to repair the broken tap.

repeat *verb*
repeats, repeating, repeated

If you **repeat** something, you say it, write it, or do it again.
Please can you repeat the question?

reply *verb*
replies, replying, replied

If you **reply** to something, give an answer.
Will you please reply when I ask you a question?

reptile *noun*
reptiles
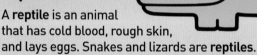

A **reptile** is an animal that has cold blood, rough skin, and lays eggs. Snakes and lizards are **reptiles**.

rescue *verb*
rescues, rescuing, rescued

If you **rescue** someone, you help them get away from a dangerous place.

rest *verb*
rests, resting, rested

If you **rest**, you sit or lie down and do not do anything active for a while.
Hello Kitty rests in the afternoon.

rest *noun*

The **rest** is the parts of something that are left.
Who ate the rest of the cake?

restaurant *noun*
restaurants

A **restaurant** is a place where you can buy and eat a meal.

result *noun*
results

A **result** is something that happens because another thing has happened.
I got measles and as a result was off school for two weeks.

return *verb*
returns, returning, returned

1 When you **return** to a place, you go back to it after you have been away.
   He returned to Japan after his holiday.

2 If you **return** something to someone, you give it back to them.
   Hello Kitty forgot to return her library books.

reward *noun*
rewards

A **reward** is something that is given to a person because they have done something good.

rhinoceros *noun*
rhinoceroses

A **rhinoceros** is a large wild animal with thick grey skin. It has one or two horns on its nose.

rhyme *verb*
rhymes, rhyming, rhymed

If two words **rhyme**, they have the same sound at the end of them.
Sally rhymes with valley.

rhythm *noun*
rhythms

Rhythm is something which is repeated again and again in the same way.
Listen to the rhythm of the music.

rib *noun*
ribs

Your **ribs** are the 12 pairs of curved bones that go round your body.
He fell off his bike and broke a rib.

ribbon *noun*
ribbons

A **ribbon** is a long narrow piece of cloth. You use **ribbons** to decorate things or tie them together.

rice *noun*

Rice is white or brown grains from a plant. **Rice** grows in wet areas.
The meal was chicken, rice, and vegetables.

rich *adjective*
richer, richest

Someone who is **rich** has a lot of money and expensive things.
She is a rich woman who owns a very large house.

riddle *noun*
riddles

A **riddle** is a question that seems to be nonsense, but that has a clever answer.
He asked the riddle, "What key cannot open a door?" and I answered, "A monkey".

a b c d e f g h i j k l m n o p q r s t u v w x y z

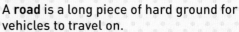

ride verb
rides, riding, rode, ridden

When you **ride** a horse or a bike, you sit on it and control it as it moves along.
Hello Kitty wants to ride her bike on the beach.

right adjective

1 If something is **right**, it is correct and there have been no mistakes.
Only Hello Kitty knew the right answer to the teacher's question.

2 The **right** side is the side that is towards the east when you look north.
Most people write with their right hand.

ring verb
rings, ringing, rang, rung

When a bell **rings**, it makes a clear, loud sound.
The alarm clock rings at seven o'clock.

ring noun
rings

A **ring** is a round piece of metal that you wear on a finger.
She turned the ring on her finger.

ripe adjective
riper, ripest

When fruit or grain is **ripe**, it is ready to be eaten.
Don't eat the apples until they are ripe.

rise verb
rises, rising, rose, risen

If something **rises**, it moves up.
Hello Kitty watched the balloon rise into the sky.

river noun
rivers

A **river** is a long line of water that flows into the sea.
The Nile is one of the longest rivers in the world.

road noun
roads

A **road** is a long piece of hard ground for vehicles to travel on.
You must look both ways before you cross the road.

roar verb
roars, roaring, roared

If a person, an animal or a thing **roars**, they make a very loud noise.
The engines roared and the aeroplane started to move.

robot noun
robots

A **robot** is a machine that can move and do things that it has been told to do.
We have robots that we could send to the moon.

rock noun
rocks

1 **Rock** is the hard material that is in the ground and in mountains.
We tried to dig, but the ground was solid rock.

2 A **rock** is a piece of this material.
Hello Kitty picked up a rock and threw it into the lake.

rock verb
rocks, rocking, rocked

If something **rocks**, it moves from side to side.

rocket *noun*
rockets

A **rocket** is a vehicle that people use to travel into space.
This is the rocket that took them to the moon.

rode

💜 Look at **ride**
Hello Kitty rode her bike down the hill.

roll *verb*
rolls, rolling, rolled

When something **rolls**, it moves along a surface, turning over and over.
Hello Kitty's ball bounced out of the garden and rolled across the road.

roof *noun*
roofs

The **roof** of a building is the bit on top that covers it.
Hello Kitty's house is the one with the red roof.

room *noun*
rooms

1 A **room** is a part of a building that has its own walls.
A minute later Hello Kitty left the room.

2 If there is **room** somewhere, there is enough empty space.
There isn't room for any more furniture in here.

root *noun*
roots

The **roots** of a plant are the parts of it that grow under the ground.
Hello Kitty dug a hole near the roots of a tree.

rope *noun*
ropes

A **rope** is a type of very thick string that is made by twisting together several strings or wires.
He tied the rope around his waist.

rose *noun*
roses

A **rose** is a large garden flower with a lovely smell. **Roses** grow on bushes.
The teacher was given a bunch of red roses.

rough *adjective*
rougher, roughest

1 If something is **rough**, it is not smooth or even.
His hands were rough.

2 If you are **rough**, you are not being careful or gentle.
Don't be so rough or you'll break it.

round *adjective*
rounder, roundest

Something **round** is in the shape of a ball or a circle.
There was a round table in the middle of the room.

row *noun*
rows

A **row** is a line of things or people.
Hello Kitty's house is opposite a row of shops.

rub *verb*
rubs, rubbing, rubbed

If you **rub** something, you move your hand or a cloth backwards and forwards over it.
Hello Kitty rubbed the window and looked outside.

rubber *noun*
rubbers

1 **Rubber** is a strong material that stretches. **Rubber** is used to make things like tyres and boots for wet weather.

2 A **rubber** is a small piece of rubber used to remove pencil mistakes.
Have you got a rubber in your pencil case?

rubbish noun

Rubbish is things like empty packs and used paper that you throw away.

rude adjective
ruder, rudest

If people are **rude**, they are not polite.
*It is **rude** to ask for something without saying "please".*

ruin verb
ruins, ruining, ruined

If you **ruin** something, you destroy or spoil it.
*The rain **ruined** the party.*

rule noun
rules

Rules are instructions that tell you what you must do or must not do.
*Can you explain the **rules** of cricket to me?*

rule verb
rules, ruling, ruled

Someone who **rules** a country controls it.

ruler noun
rulers

1 A **ruler** is a long, flat piece of wood or plastic with straight edges. You use a **ruler** for measuring things or drawing straight lines.

2 A **ruler** is also a person who rules a country. *He was **ruler** of France at that time.*

run verb
runs, running, ran, run

When you **run**, you move very quickly on your legs.
*It's very dangerous to **run** across the road.*

rung

♥ Look at **ring**
*They had **rung** the door bell when I was in the shower.*

sad adjective
sadder, saddest

If you are **sad**, you don't feel happy.
*Hello Kitty is **sad** that her friend is leaving.*

safe adjective
safer, safest

If you are **safe**, you are not in any danger.
*Is it **safe**?*

said

♥ Look at **say**
*That is what she **said** to Hello Kitty.*

sail noun
sails

Sails are large pieces of cloth on a boat that catch the wind and move the boat along.

salad noun
salads

A **salad** is a mixture of vegetables and sometimes other foods. You usually eat **salads** cold.

salt noun

Salt is a white powder that you use to make food taste better.
*Now add **salt** and pepper.*

same adjective

If two things are the **same**, they are like one another.
The two cats look the same.

sand noun

Sand is a powder made of very small pieces of stone.
Deserts and most beaches are made of **sand**.

sandal noun
sandals

Sandals are light shoes that you wear in warm weather.
Hello Kitty has a new pair of sandals.

sandwich noun
sandwiches

A **sandwich** is two slices of bread with another food such as cheese or meat between them.
My sister had a sandwich for lunch.

sang

♥ Look at **sing**
Hello Kitty sang a happy song.

sank

♥ Look at **sink**
The boat sank in the storm.

sari noun
saris

A **sari** is a long piece of material worn folded around the body by women.
She was wearing a new yellow sari.

sat

♥ Look at **sit**
Hello Kitty sat down next to her friend.

satellite noun
satellites

A **satellite** is a machine that is sent into space to receive and send back information.

Saturday noun
Saturdays

Saturday is the day after Friday and before Sunday.
I met Hello Kitty on Saturday morning.

saucepan noun
saucepans

A **saucepan** is a deep metal container with a long handle and a lid. **Saucepans** are used for cooking.
Put the potatoes in a saucepan and boil them.

saucer noun
saucers

A **saucer** is a small curved plate that you put under a cup.

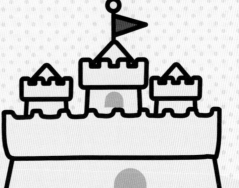

a
b
c
d
e
f
g
h
i
j
k
l
m
n
o
p
q
r
s
t
u
v
w
x
y
z

sausage *noun*
sausages

A **sausage** is a mixture of very small pieces of meat and other foods, inside a long thin skin.

save *verb*
saves, saving, saved

1 If you **save** someone or something, you help them to escape from danger.
   He saved the boy from drowning.

2 If you **save** something, you keep it because you will need it later.
   Hello Kitty is saving her money.

saw

♥ Look at **see**
Hello Kitty saw her walking down the street.

saw *noun*
saws

A **saw** is a metal tool for cutting wood.
He used a saw to cut the branches off the tree.

say *verb*
says, saying, said

When you **say** something, you talk.
My friend says she is very hungry.

scale *noun*
scales

Scales are small, flat pieces of hard skin that cover the body of animals like fish and snakes.

scales *noun*

Scales are a machine used for weighing things.
He weighed flour on the scales.

scared *adjective*

If you are **scared** of something it frightens you.
She is scared of spiders.

school *noun*
schools

A **school** is a place where people go to learn.
The school was built in the 1960s.

science *noun*
sciences

Science is the study of natural things.

scissors *noun*

Scissors are a small tool for cutting with two sharp parts that are joined together.
Cut the card using scissors.

score *verb*
scores, scoring, scored

If you **score** in a game, you get a goal, run, or point.
He scored his second goal of the game.

scratch *verb*
scratches, scratching, scratched

1 If a sharp thing **scratches** someone or something, it makes small cuts on their skin or on its surface.
   The branches scratched my face.

2 If you **scratch** part of your body, you rub your nails against your skin.
   Hello Kitty scratched her head.

A B C D E F G H I J K L M N O P Q R S T U V W X Y Z

scream *verb*
screams, screaming, screamed

If you **scream**, you shout or cry in a loud, high voice.
She screamed when she saw the spider.

screen *noun*
screens

A **screen** is a flat surface on which a picture is shown.
There was dust on the television screen.

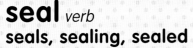

sea *noun*
seas

A **sea** is a large area of salt water.
Hello Kitty swam in the warm sea.

seal *verb*
seals, sealing, sealed

When you **seal** an envelope, you close it by folding part of it and sticking it down.
Hello Kitty sealed the envelope and put on a stamp.

search *verb*
searches, searching, searched

If you **search** for something or someone, you look for them everywhere.
Hello Kitty is searching for her bag.

seaside *noun*

The **seaside** is an area next to the sea.
Hello Kitty went to spend a day at the seaside.

season *noun*
seasons

The **seasons** are the four parts of a year: spring, summer, autumn and winter.
Autumn is my favourite season.

seat *noun*
seats

A **seat** is something that you can sit on.

second *adjective*

The **second** thing in a number of things is the one that you count as number two.
It was the second day of Hello Kitty's holiday.

second *noun*
seconds

A **second** is an amount of time. There are sixty **seconds** in one minute.
For a few seconds nobody spoke.

secret *adjective*

If something is **secret**, only a small number of people know about it, and they do not tell any other people.
Hello Kitty had a secret place to hide in the garden.

see *verb*
sees, seeing, saw, seen

1   If you **see** something, you are looking at it or you notice it.
    The fog was so thick Hello Kitty couldn't see anything.

2   If you **see** someone, you meet them.
    Hello Kitty saw him yesterday.

seed *noun*
seeds

A **seed** is the small, hard part of a plant from which a new plant grows.
Plant the seeds in the garden.

seem *verb*
seems, seeming, seemed

If something **seems** to be true, it appears to be true or you think it is true.
The thunder seemed very close.

117

seen

💜 Look at **see**
*Hello Kitty had **seen** the film before.*

sell *verb*
sells, selling, sold

If you **sell** something, you let someone have it in return for money.
*The man **sold** his bike.*

semicircle *noun*
semicircles

A **semicircle** is a half of a circle, or something with this shape.
*The children stood in a **semicircle**.*

send *verb*
sends, sending, sent

When you **send** someone a message or a parcel, you make it go to them.
*I will **send** you a letter when I arrive.*

sensible *adjective*

If you do something **sensible**, you have thought about it a lot first.
*The **sensible** thing is not to touch it.*

sent

💜 Look at **send**
*Hello Kitty **sent** a letter home.*

September *noun*

September is the month after August and before October.
It has 30 days.

serve *verb*
serves, serving, served

Someone who **serves** customers in a shop or a restaurant helps them with what they want to buy.
*She **served** me coffee and cake.*

set *noun*
sets

A **set** of things is a number of things that belong together.
*Hello Kitty needs a **set** of clean clothes.*

seven *noun*

Seven is the number **7**.

several *adjective*

You use **several** for talking about a number of people or things that is not large but is greater than two.
*There were **several** boxes on the table.*

sew *verb*
sews, sewing, sewed, sewn

When you **sew** pieces of cloth together, you join them using a needle and thread.
*I must **sew** a button on to this shirt.*

sex *noun*
sexes

The **sex** of a person or animal is if it is male or female.
*What **sex** is the baby?*

shadow *noun*
shadows

A **shadow** is a dark shape on a surface that is made when something blocks the light.
*The **shadows** of the trees crossed their path.*

shake *verb*
shakes, shaking, shook, shaken

1 If you **shake** something, you hold it and move it quickly up and down.
* **Shake** the bottle before you drink.*

2 If someone or something **shakes**, they move quickly backwards and forwards or up and down.
* My body was **shaking** with cold.*

shallow *adjective*
shallower, shallowest

If something is **shallow**, it is not deep.
*The river is very **shallow** here.*

shape *noun*
shapes

The **shape** of something is the way its outside edges or surfaces look.
*Pasta comes in different **shapes** and sizes.*

share *verb*
shares, sharing, shared

If you **share** something with another person, you both have it or use it.
*Hello Kitty **shared** her pencils with me.*

shark *noun*
sharks

A **shark** is a very large fish. **Sharks** have very sharp teeth and some may attack people.

sharp *adjective*
sharper, sharpest

1 A **sharp** point or edge is very thin and can cut through things quickly.
* Be careful, the scissors are **sharp**.*

2 A **sharp** feeling is sudden and is very big or strong.
* I felt a **sharp** pain in my right leg.*

shave *verb*
shaves, shaving, shaved

If you **shave**, you remove hair from your face or body by cutting it off.
*Samuel took a bath and **shaved**.*

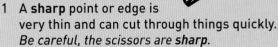

shed *noun*
sheds

A **shed** is a small building where you store things.
*The house has a large **shed** in the garden.*

she'd

1 **She'd** is short for **she had**.
* **She'd** already seen them.*

2 **She'd** is also short for **she would**.
* **She'd** be very happy to see you.*

sheep *noun*
sheep

A **sheep** is a farm animal with thick hair called wool. Farmers keep **sheep** for their wool or for their meat.

sheet *noun*
sheets

1 A **sheet** is a large piece of cloth that you sleep on or cover yourself with in bed.
* Once a week, we change the **sheets**.*

2 A **sheet** is a piece of paper, glass, plastic, or metal.
* Hello Kitty folded the **sheets** of paper.*

shelf noun
shelves

A **shelf** is a long flat piece of wood on a wall or in a cupboard that you can keep things on.
Hello Kitty took a book from the shelf.

shell noun
shells

1   The **shell** of an egg or nut is its hard part.
2   The **shell** of an animal such as a snail is the hard part that covers its back and protects it.

she'll

She'll is short for **she will**.
She'll be back.

she's

She's is short for **she is**.
She's a doctor.

shine verb
shines, shining, shone

If something **shines**, it gives out bright light.
Today it's warm and the sun is shining.

shiny adjective
shinier, shiniest

If something is **shiny**, it is bright.
Her hair was shiny and clean.

ship noun
ships

A **ship** is a large boat that carries people or things.
The ship was ready to leave.

shirt noun
shirts

A **shirt** is something you wear on the top part of your body. It has a collar and buttons.

shiver verb
shivers, shivering, shivered

If you **shiver**, your body shakes because you are cold or scared.
She shivered with cold.

shoe noun
shoes

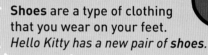

Shoes are a type of clothing that you wear on your feet.
Hello Kitty has a new pair of shoes.

shone

♥ Look at **shine**
The sun shone all day.

shop noun
shops

A **shop** is a place that sells things.
Hello Kitty went to the shop to buy some bread.

A B C D E F G H I J K L M N O P Q R S T U V W X Y Z

shore *noun*
shores

The **shore** of a sea or lake is the land along the edge of it.
*Hello Kitty walked slowly down to the **shore**.*

short *adjective*
shorter, shortest

1 If something is **short**, it does not last very long.
   *Last year Hello Kitty went to the seaside for a **short** holiday.*

2 A **short** thing is small in length, distance, or height.
   *She has **short**, straight hair.*

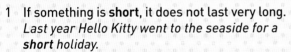

shorts *noun*

Shorts are trousers with short legs.
*Hello Kitty was wearing blue **shorts**.*

should *verb*

You use **should** when you are saying what is the right thing to do.
*He **should** tell us what happened.*

shoulder *noun*
shoulders

Your **shoulders** are the two parts of your body between your neck and the tops of your arms.
*Put your hands on the **shoulders** of the person in front of you.*

shout *verb*
shouts, shouting, shouted

If you **shout**, you say something in a very loud voice.
*He **shouted** something to his brother.*

show *verb*
shows, showing, showed, shown

1 If you **show** someone something, you let them see it.
   *Hello Kitty **showed** me her new crayons.*

2 If you **show** someone how to do something, you teach them how to do it.
   *She **showed** us how to make pasta.*

shower *noun*
showers

1 A **shower** is a thing that you stand under, that covers you with water so you can wash yourself.
   *I was in the **shower** when the phone rang.*

2 A **shower** is a short period of rain.
   *A few **showers** are expected tomorrow.*

shown

♥ Look at **show**
*I've **shown** Hello Kitty how to do it.*

shut *verb*
shuts, shutting, shut

If you **shut** something, you close it.
*Hello Kitty **shut** the gate.*

shy *adjective*
shyer, shyest

If you are **shy**, you are nervous about talking to people that you do not know well.
*She was a **shy**, quiet girl.*

sick *adjective*
sicker, sickest

If you are **sick**, you are not well.
*He's very **sick** and needs a doctor.*

side *noun*
sides

1 The **side** of something is a place to the left or right of it.
   *On the left **side** of the door there's a door bell.*

2 The **side** of something is also its edge.
   *A square has four **sides**.*

3 The different **sides** in a game are the groups of people who are playing against each other.
   *Both **sides** want to win the match.*

A B C D E F G H I J K L M N O P Q R **S** ✿ T U V W X Y Z

sign *noun*
signs

1 A **sign** is a mark or a shape that has a special meaning.
*In maths, + is a plus **sign** and - is a minus **sign**.*

2 You can also make a **sign** to somebody by moving something.
*They gave me a **sign** to show that everything was all right.*

silent *adjective*

1 If you are **silent**, you are not talking.
*She was **silent** because she did not know what to say.*

2 If something is **silent**, it is quiet, with no sound at all.
*The room was **silent**.*

silly *adjective*
sillier, silliest

If you are **silly**, you do not behave in a sensible way.
*Don't be **silly**!*

silver *noun*

Silver is a valuable metal.
*Hello Kitty has a bracelet made from **silver**.*

sing *verb*
sings, singing, sang, sung

When you **sing**, you make music with your voice.
*I love to **sing** in the bath.*

sink *noun*
sinks

A **sink** is a large fixed container in a kitchen or a bathroom that you can fill with water.
*The **sink** was filled with dirty dishes.*

sink *verb*
sinks, sinking, sank, sunk

If a boat **sinks**, it goes below the surface of the water.
*The boat hit the rocks and began to **sink**.*

sister *noun*
sisters

Your **sister** is a girl or woman who has the same parents as you.
*This is my **sister**.*

sit *verb*
sits, sitting, sat

If you are **sitting** in a chair, your bottom is resting on the chair and the top part of your body is straight.
*Hello Kitty was **sitting** in a chair in the kitchen.*

six *noun*

Six is the number **6**.

size *noun*
sizes

The **size** of something is how big or small it is.
*The **size** of the room is about five metres by seven metres.*

skate *noun*
skates

Skates are boots with a thin metal bar on the bottom for moving quickly on ice.

skeleton *noun*
skeletons

A **skeleton** is all the bones in a person's or animal's body.
*A human **skeleton** has more than 200 bones.*

skies

♥ Look at **sky**
*The **skies** were grey.*

skill *noun*

If you have **skill** you are able to do something well.
*He shows great **skill** on the football field.*

skin *noun*
skins

1 Your **skin** covers your whole body.
Too much sun can damage your skin.

2 The **skin** of a fruit or vegetable covers the outside of it.
She slipped on a banana skin.

skip *verb*
skips, skipping, skipped

1 If you **skip** along, you move along jumping from one foot to the other.
Hello Kitty skipped down the street.

2 If you **skip** something, you decide not to do it.
Don't skip breakfast.

skirt *noun*
skirts

A **skirt** is something that women and girls wear. It hangs down from the waist and covers part of the legs.

skull *noun*
skulls

A person's or animal's **skull** is the bones of their head.
Your skull protects your brain.

sky *noun*
skies

The **sky** is the space around the Earth which you can see when you look up.
The sun was shining in the sky.

sleep *verb*
sleeps, sleeping, slept

If you **sleep**, you rest with your eyes closed and you do not move.
Be quiet! The baby is sleeping.

sleeve *noun*
sleeves

The **sleeves** of something you wear are the parts that cover your arms.
Hello Kitty wore a blue dress with long sleeves.

slept

♥ Look at **sleep**
Hello Kitty slept for three hours.

slice *noun*
slices

A **slice** of something is a thin piece that you cut from a larger piece.
Would you like a slice of bread?

slide *verb*
slides, sliding, slid

When someone or something **slides**, they move quickly over a surface.
He slid down the hill on the ice.

slip *verb*
slips, slipping, slipped

If you **slip**, you slide and fall.
He slipped on the wet grass.

slipper *noun*
slippers

Slippers are loose, soft shoes that you wear indoors.
Hello Kitty put on a pair of slippers.

slippery *adjective*

If something is **slippery**, it is smooth or wet, and is difficult to walk on or to hold.
*Be careful – the floor is **slippery**.*

slope *noun*
slopes

A **slope** is the side of a mountain, hill, or valley.
*A steep **slope** leads to the beach.*

slow *adjective*
slower, slowest

If something is **slow**, it does not move quickly.
*The bus was very **slow**.*

slowly

If something moves **slowly**, it does not move quickly.

slug *noun*
slugs

A **slug** is a small animal with a long soft body and no legs that moves very slowly.

small *adjective*
smaller, smallest

If something is **small**, it is not large in size or amount.
*She is **small** for her age.*

smash *verb*
smashes, smashing, smashed

If you **smash** something, it breaks into many pieces.
*The plate **smashed** when it hit the floor.*

smell *noun*
smells

The **smell** of something is what you notice about it when you breathe in through your nose.
*There was a horrible **smell** in the fridge.*

smile *verb*
smiles, smiling, smiled

If you **smile**, the corners of your mouth turn up because you are happy or you think that something is funny.
*The little boy **smiled** at his mum.*

smoke *noun*

Smoke is the black or white clouds of gas that you see in the air when something burns.
*Thick black **smoke** blew over the city.*

smooth *adjective*
smoother, smoothest

Something **smooth** has no rough parts, lumps, or holes.
*The baby's skin was soft and **smooth**.*

snail *noun*
snails

A **snail** is a small animal with a long, soft body, no legs, and a round shell on its back.

snake noun
snakes

A **snake** is a long, thin animal with no legs, that slides along the ground.

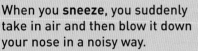

sneeze verb
sneezes, sneezing, sneezed

When you **sneeze**, you suddenly take in air and then blow it down your nose in a noisy way.
Cover your nose and mouth when you sneeze.

snow noun

Snow is pieces of soft white frozen water that fall from the sky.
Six inches of snow fell last night.

soap noun

Soap is something that you use with water for washing yourself.
She bought a bar of soap.

sock
socks noun

Socks are pieces of cloth that you wear over your foot and ankle, inside your shoes.
Hello Kitty has a pair of red socks.

sofa noun
sofas

A **sofa** is a long, comfortable seat with a back, that two or three people can sit on.

soft adjective
softer, softest

1 Something that is **soft** is nice to touch, and not rough or hard.
   She wiped the baby's face with a soft cloth.

2 A **soft** sound or light is very gentle.
   There was a soft tapping on my door.

soil noun

Soil is the top layer on the surface of the earth in which plants grow.
The soil here is good for growing vegetables.

sold

♥ Look at **sell**
They sold their house today.

soldier noun
soldiers

A **soldier** is someone who is in an army.

solid adjective

1 Something that is **solid** stays the same shape if it is in a container or not.

2 Something that is **solid** is not hollow.
   They had to cut through 5 feet of solid rock.

some

You use **some** to talk about an amount of something.
Can I have some orange juice, please?

somebody

You use **somebody** to talk about a person without saying who you mean.

someone

You use **someone** to talk about a person without saying who you mean.
I need someone to help me.

something

You use **something** to talk about a thing without saying what it is.
He knew that there was something wrong.

sometimes

You use **sometimes** to talk about things that do not take place all the time.
Sometimes he's a little rude.

a b c d e f g h i j k l m n o p q r **s** t u v w x y z

A B C D E F G H I J K L M N O P Q R **S** ❀ T U V W X Y Z

somewhere

You use **somewhere** to talk about a place without saying where you mean.
Hello Kitty has seen her before somewhere.

son *noun*
sons

Someone's **son** is their male child.
His son is his seven years old.

song *noun*
songs

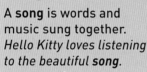

A **song** is words and music sung together.
Hello Kitty loves listening to the beautiful song.

soon
sooner, soonest

If you are going to do something **soon** you will do it a very short time from now.
I'll call you soon.

sore *adjective*
sorer, sorest

If part of your body is **sore**, it is painful.
I had a sore throat.

sorry *adjective*
sorrier, sorriest

1   If you are **sorry** about something, you feel sad about it.
    Hello Kitty is sorry he's gone.

2   If you feel **sorry** for someone, you feel sad for them.
    Hello Kitty felt sorry for him because nobody listened to him.

sort *noun*
sorts

The different **sorts** of something are the different types of it.
What sort of school do you go to?

sound *noun*
sounds

A **sound** is something that you hear.
He heard the sound of a car engine outside.

soup *noun*

Soup is liquid food made by boiling meat, fish, or vegetables in water.

sour *adjective*

Something that is **sour** has a sharp, nasty taste.
Lemons have a sour taste.

south *noun*

The **south** is the direction to your right when you are looking towards the place where the sun rises.

space *noun*
spaces

1   You use **space** to talk about an area that is empty.
    They cut down trees to make space for houses.

2   **Space** is the area past the Earth, where the stars and planets are.
    The six astronauts will spend ten days in space.

spade *noun*
spades

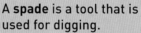

A **spade** is a tool that is used for digging.

speak *verb*
speaks, speaking, spoken

When you **speak**, you say words.
The man speaks in a very loud voice.

special *adjective*

Someone or something that is **special** is better or more important than other people or things.
Mum made a special card for Hello Kitty's birthday.

speed *noun*
speeds

The **speed** of something is how fast it moves or is done.
He rode off at high speed.

spell *verb*
spells, spelling, spelled or **spelt**

When you **spell** a word, you write or say each letter in the correct order.
Hello Kitty spelled her name.

spend *verb*
spends, spending, spent

1 When you **spend** money, you buy things with it.
I have spent all my money.

2 To **spend** time or energy is to use it doing something.
She spends hours working on her garden.

spider *noun*
spiders

A **spider** is a small animal with eight legs.

spill *verb*
spills, spilling, spilled or **spilt**

If you **spill** a liquid, you make it flow over the edge of a container by accident.
He always spilled the drinks.

spin *verb*
spins, spinning, spun

If something **spins**, it turns around quickly.
He made the coin spin on his desk.

spine *noun*
spines

Your **spine** is the row of bones down your back.

splash *verb*
splashes, splashing, splashed

If you **splash** in water, you hit the water in a noisy way.
Hello Kitty splashed in the water.

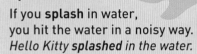

spoil *verb*
spoils, spoiling, spoiled or **spoilt**

1 If you **spoil** something, you damage it or stop it from working as it should.
Don't spoil the surprise.

2 If you **spoil** children, you give them everything they want or ask for.
She acted like a spoilt child.

a b c d e f g h i j k l m n o p q r s t u v w x y z

spoke *noun*
spokes

The **spokes** of a wheel are the bars which join the outside ring to the centre.

spoke

💜 Look at **speak**
*The little girl **spoke** very quietly.*

spoken

💜 Look at **speak**
*I have **spoken** to all my friends today.*

spoon *noun*
spoons

A **spoon** is a long tool with a round end that is used for eating, serving or mixing food.
*He stirred his coffee with a **spoon**.*

sport *noun*
sports

Sports are games which need energy and skill.
*Hello Kitty is very good at **sport**.*

spot *noun*
spots

Spots are small, round areas on a surface.
*The leaves are yellow with orange **spots**.*

spot *verb*
spots, spotting, spotted

If you **spot** something or someone, you notice them.
*I didn't **spot** the mistake in his work.*

spout *noun*
spouts

A **spout** is a tube for pouring liquid.
*My kettle has a long **spout**.*

spray *noun*
sprays

Spray is a lot of small drops of water that are thrown into the air.
*The **spray** from the waves covered them.*

spread *verb*
spreads, spreading, spread

1 If you **spread** something somewhere, you open it out.
   *Hello Kitty **spread** a towel on the sand and lay on it.*

2 If you **spread** something on a surface, you put it all over the surface.
   *Hello Kitty was **spreading** butter on the bread.*

3 If something **spreads**, it reaches a larger area.
   *The news **spread** quickly.*

spring *noun*
springs

1 **Spring** is the season between winter and summer when the weather becomes warmer and plants start to grow again.
   *They are getting married next **spring**.*

2 A **spring** is a long piece of metal that goes round and round. It goes back to the same shape after you pull it.
   *The **springs** in the bed were old.*

spun

💜 Look at **spin**
*He **spun** the wheel.*

square noun
squares

A **square** is a shape with four straight sides that are all the same length.
*Cut the cake in **squares**.*

squirrel noun
squirrels

A **squirrel** is a small animal with a long thick tail. **Squirrels** live in trees.

stable noun
stables

A **stable** is a building where people keep horses.

stairs noun

Stairs are steps you walk down or up in a building.
*Hello Kitty walked up the **stairs**.*

stamp noun
stamps

A **stamp** is a small piece of paper that you stick on an envelope before you post it.
*Hello Kitty put a **stamp** on the corner of the envelope.*

stamp verb
stamps, stamping, stamped

If you **stamp** your foot, you put your foot down very hard on the ground.
*Hello Kitty **stamped** her feet to keep warm.*

stand verb
stands, standing, stood

When you are **standing**, you are on your feet.
*Hello Kitty was **standing** beside my bed.*

star noun
stars

1 A **star** is a large ball of burning gas in space. **Stars** look like small points of light in the sky.
   Stars lit the sky.

2 A **star** is a shape that has four, five, or more points sticking out of it in a pattern.
   *How many **stars** are there on the flag?*

3 A **star** is somebody who is famous for doing something, for example acting or singing.
   *He's one of the **stars** of a TV show.*

start verb
starts, starting, started

1 When something **starts**, it begins.
   *When does the film **start**?*

2 If you **start** to do something, you begin to do it.
   *Hello Kitty **started** to read her book.*

station noun
stations

A **station** is a place where trains or buses stop so that people can get on or off.
*Hello Kitty walked to the bus **station**.*

stay verb
stays, staying, stayed

1 If you **stay** in a place, you do not move away from it.
   *She **stayed** in bed until noon.*

2 If you **stay** somewhere, you live there for a short time.
   *He **stayed** with them for two weeks.*

steady adjective
steadier, steadiest

Something that is **steady** is firm and not shaking.
*Hello Kitty held out a **steady** hand.*

steal verb
steals, stealing, stole, stolen

If you **steal** something from someone, you take it without asking them and don't give it back.
*They said he **stole** a bicycle.*

a
b
c
d
e
f
g
h
i
j
k
l
m
n
o
p
q
r
s
t
u
v
w
x
y
z

steam *noun*

Steam is the hot gas that water becomes when it boils.
*The **steam** rose into the air.*

steel *noun*

Steel is a very strong metal that is made from iron.
*The door is made of **steel.***

steep *adjective*
steeper, steepest

A **steep** slope rises quickly and is difficult to go up.
*Some of the hills are very **steep.***

stem *noun*
stems

The **stem** of a plant is the long, thin part that the flowers and leaves grow on.
*He cut the **stem** and gave Hello Kitty the flower.*

step *noun*
steps

1 If you take a **step**, you lift your foot and put it down in a different place.
   *Hello Kitty took a **step** towards him.*

2 A **step** is a flat surface that you put your feet on to walk up or down to somewhere.
   *Hello Kitty went down the **steps** into the garden.*

stick *noun*
sticks

A **stick** is a long, thin piece of wood.
*She put some dry **sticks** on the fire.*

stick *verb*
sticks, sticking, stuck

If you **stick** one thing to another, you join them together using glue.
*Now **stick** your picture on a piece of paper.*

stiff *adjective*
stiffer, stiffest

Something that is **stiff** is firm and is not easy to bend.
*The sheet of cardboard was **stiff.***

still *adjective*
stiller, stillest

If you are **still**, you are not moving.
*Please stand **still.***

sting *verb*
stings, stinging, stung

If a plant, an animal, or an insect **stings** you, a part of it is pushed into your skin so that you feel a sharp pain.
*She was **stung** by a wasp.*

stir *verb*
stirs, stirring, stirred

When you **stir** a liquid, you move it around using a spoon or a stick.

stole

♥ Look at **steal**
*They **stole** our car last night.*

stolen

♥ Look at **steal**
*All of her money was **stolen.***

stomach *noun*
stomachs

Your **stomach** is the place inside your body where food goes when you eat it.
*My **stomach** felt full after the meal.*

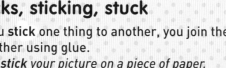

A B C D E F G H I J K L M N O P Q R S T U V W X Y Z

stone *noun*
stones

1   **Stone** is a hard solid material that is found in the ground. It is often used for building.
*The floor was solid **stone**.*

2   A **stone** is a small piece of rock that is found on the ground.
*Hello Kitty took a **stone** out of her shoe.*

stood

💜 Look at **stand**
*Hello Kitty **stood** in the street.*

stop *verb*
stops, stopping, stopped

1   If you **stop** doing something, you do not do it any more.
***Stop** throwing those stones!*

2   If something **stops**, it does not do what it did any more.
*The rain has **stopped**.*

store *verb*
stores, storing, stored

If you **store** something, you keep it somewhere safe.

storm *noun*
storms

A **storm** is very bad weather, with heavy rain and strong winds.
*There will be **storms** along the East Coast.*

story *noun*
stories

When someone tells you a **story** they describe people and things that are not real, in a way that makes you enjoy hearing about them.
*Hello Kitty loves to hear a **story** at bedtime.*

straight *adjective*
straighter, straightest

If something is **straight**, it goes one way and does not bend.
*The boat moved in a **straight** line.*

strange *adjective*
stranger, strangest

Something that is **strange** is unusual.
*I had a **strange** dream last night.*

straw *noun*
straws

1   **Straw** is the dry, yellow stems of crops.
*The floor of the barn was covered with **straw**.*

2   A **straw** is a thin tube that you use to suck a drink into your mouth.
*I drank my milk through a pink **straw**.*

strawberry *noun*
strawberries

A **strawberry** is a small soft red fruit that has a lot of very small seeds on its skin.

stream *noun*
streams

A **stream** is a small narrow river.
*There was a **stream** at the end of the garden.*

a b c d e f g h i j k l m n o p q r **s** t u v w x y z

street noun
streets

A **street** is a road in a city or a town.
*We live in a lovely **street**.*

strength noun

Your **strength** is how strong you are.
*Swimming builds up the **strength** of your muscles.*

stretch verb
stretches, stretching, stretched

1 Something that **stretches** over an area
   covers all of it.
   *The line of cars **stretched** for miles.*

2 When you **stretch**, you hold out part of your
   body as far as you can.
   *Every morning Hello Kitty **stretches** her arms.*

strict adjective
stricter, strictest

A **strict** person expects people to obey rules.
*My parents are very **strict**.*

string noun
strings

1 **String** is thin rope made of twisted threads.
   *Hello Kitty held out a small bag tied
   with **string**.*

2 The **strings** on an instrument are
   the thin pieces of wire that are
   stretched across it and that
   make sounds when the
   instrument is played.
   *He changed a guitar **string**.*

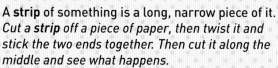

strip noun
strips

A **strip** of something is a long, narrow piece of it.
*Cut a **strip** off a piece of paper, then twist it and
stick the two ends together. Then cut it along the
middle and see what happens.*

stripe noun
stripes

A **stripe** is a long line that is a different colour
from the areas next to it.
*Hello Kitty wore a blue skirt with white **stripes**.*

strong adjective
stronger, strongest

1 Someone who is **strong** is healthy with good
   muscles.
   *I'm not **strong** enough to carry him.*

2 **Strong** things are not easy to break.
   *This **strong** plastic will not crack.*

stuck adjective

1 If something is **stuck** in a place, it cannot move.
   *His car got **stuck** in the snow.*

2 If you get **stuck**, you can't go on doing
   something because it is too difficult.
   *The teacher will help if you get **stuck**.*

stung

♥ Look at **sting**
*He was **stung** by a bee.*

submarine noun
submarines

A **submarine** is a ship that can travel under the
sea.

subtraction noun

Subtraction is when you take one number away
from another.

suck verb
sucks, sucking, sucked

If you **suck** something, you hold it in your mouth
for a long time.
*How long can you **suck** the sweet for?*

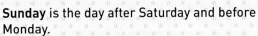

sudden *adjective*

Something **sudden** is quick and is not expected.
The car came to a sudden stop.

suddenly

Suddenly is quickly, without being expected.
Suddenly there was a loud bang.

sugar *noun*

Sugar is a sweet thing that is used for making food and drinks taste sweet.
Do you take sugar in your coffee?

suit *noun*
suits

A **suit** is a jacket and trousers or a skirt that are made from the same cloth.
He was wearing a blue suit.

sum *noun*
sums

1 A **sum** of money is an amount of money.
   Large sums of money were lost.

2 In maths, a **sum** is a problem you work out using numbers.
   Hello Kitty has to finish these sums.

summer *noun*
summers

Summer is the season after spring and before autumn. In the **summer** the weather is usually warm or hot.

sun *noun*
suns

The **sun** is the large ball of burning gas in the sky that gives us light.
The sun was now high in the sky.

Sunday *noun*
Sundays

Sunday is the day after Saturday and before Monday.
We went for a drive on Sunday.

sunflower *noun*
sunflowers

A **sunflower** is a very tall plant with large yellow flowers.

sung

💜 Look at **sing**
The children have sung this song many times.

sunk

💜 Look at **sink**
The rock has sunk to the bottom of the river.

sunny *adjective*
sunnier, sunniest

When it is **sunny**, the sun is shining.
The weather was warm and sunny.

A B C D E F G H I J K L M N O P Q R S 🌸 T U V W X Y Z

sunshine *noun*

Sunshine is the light that comes from the sun.
*Hello Kitty was sitting outside in bright **sunshine**.*

supermarket *noun*
supermarkets

A **supermarket** is a large shop that sells all kinds of food and other things for the home.
*Lots of people buy food in a **supermarket**.*

sure *adjective*

If you are **sure** that something is true, you know that it is true.
*Hello Kitty is **sure** her answer is correct.*

surface *noun*
surfaces

The **surface** of something is the flat top part of it or the outside of it.
*There were pen marks on the table's **surface**.*

surname *noun*
surnames

Your **surname** is your last name which you share with other people in your family.

surprise *noun*
surprises

A **surprise** is something that you do not expect.
*I have a **surprise** for you!*

swallow *verb*
swallows, swallowing, swallowed

If you **swallow** something, you make it go from your mouth down into your stomach.
*The boy took a bite of the apple and **swallowed** it.*

swam

💜 Look at **swim**
*Hello Kitty **swam** in the ocean.*

swan *noun*
swans

A **swan** is a large bird with a long neck, that lives on rivers and lakes.

sweep *verb*
sweeps, sweeping, swept

If you **sweep** an area, you push dirt off it using a brush with a long handle.
*The man in the shop was **sweeping** the floor.*

sweet *noun*
sweets

Sweets are foods that have a lot of sugar.
*Don't eat too many **sweets**.*

sweet adjective
sweeter, sweetest

Sweet food and drink has a lot of sugar in it.
Mum gave me a cup of sweet tea.

swept

💜 Look at **sweep**
The rubbish was swept away.

swim verb
swims, swimming, swam, swum

When you **swim**, you move through water by moving your arms and legs.
Hello Kitty learned to swim when she was three.

swing verb
swings, swinging, swung

If something **swings**, it keeps moving backwards and forwards or from side to side through the air.
Hello Kitty walked beside him with her arms swinging.

switch noun
switches

A **switch** is a small button for turning something on or off.
Hello Kitty pressed the switch to turn on the light.

sword noun
swords

A **sword** is like a long knife, with a handle and a long sharp blade.

swum

💜 Look at **swim**
Hello Kitty had never swum so far.

swung

💜 Look at **swing**
Hello Kitty swung her bag backwards and forwards.

Tt

table noun
tables

A **table** is a piece of furniture that has legs and a flat top.

tadpole noun
tadpoles

A **tadpole** is a small black animal with a round head and a long tail that lives in water. **Tadpoles** grow into frogs or toads.

tail noun
tails

An animal's **tail** is the long, thin part at the end of its body.

take verb
takes, taking, took, taken

1   If you **take** something, you move it or carry it.
    Hello Kitty took the plates into the kitchen.

2   If you **take** something that does not belong to you, you steal it.
    Someone took all our money.

3   If you **take** a vehicle, you ride in it from one place to another.
    Hello Kitty took the bus to school.

talk verb
talks, talking, talked

When you **talk**, you say things to someone.
I love to talk to my friends on the phone.

tall *adjective*
taller, tallest

If a person or thing is **tall**, they are higher than usual from top to bottom.
*It was a very **tall** building.*

tame *adjective*
tamer, tamest

If an animal or bird is **tame**, it is not afraid of people and will not try to hurt them.

tap *verb*
taps, tapping, tapped

If you **tap** something, you hit it but you do not use a lot of strength.
*Hello Kitty **tapped** on the door and went in.*

tape *noun*

Tape is a long, thin strip of plastic that has glue on one side. You use **tape** to stick things together.
*Hello Kitty wrapped the parcel with paper and **tape**.*

taste *verb*
tastes, tasting, tasted

If you **taste** something, you eat or drink a small amount of it to see what it is like.
*She **tasted** the soup and then added some salt.*

taught

♥ Look at **teach**
*My mum **taught** me to read.*

tea *noun*

1 **Tea** is a drink. You make it by pouring hot water on to the dry leaves of a plant called the **tea** bush.

2 **Tea** is also a meal that you eat in the afternoon or the early evening.

teach *verb*
teaches, teaching, taught

If you **teach** someone something, you help them to understand it or you show them how to do it.
*He **teaches** people how to play the piano.*

teacher *noun*
teachers

A **teacher** is a person whose job is to teach other people. Teachers usually work in schools.

team *noun*
teams

A **team** is a group of people who work together, or who play a sport together against another group.
*He is in the school football **team**.*

tear *noun*
tears

Tears are the liquid that comes out of your eyes when you cry.
*Her face was wet with **tears**.*

tear *verb*
tears, tearing, tore, torn

If you **tear** something, you pull it into pieces or make a hole in it.
*Try not to **tear** the paper.*

teeth

♥ Look at **tooth**
*Clean your **teeth** before you go to bed.*

telephone *noun*
telephones

A **telephone** is a machine that you use to talk to someone who is in another place.

television *noun*
televisions

A **television** is a machine that shows moving pictures with sound on a screen.

tell *verb*
tells, telling, told

1 If you **tell** someone something, you let them know about it.
Tell me about your holiday.

2 If you **tell** someone to do something, you say that they must do it.
She told me to go away.

3 If you can **tell** something, you know it.
I can tell that he is angry.

ten *noun*

Ten is the number **10**.

tent *noun*
tents

A **tent** is made of strong material that is held up with long pieces of metal and ropes. You sleep in a **tent** when you stay in a camp.

term *noun*
terms

A **term** is one of the parts of a school year. There are usually three **terms** in a year.

terrible *adjective*

If something is **terrible**, it is very bad.
That was a terrible film.

test *verb*
tests, testing, tested

If you **test** something, you try it to see what it is like, or how it works.
Test the water to see if it is warm.

test *noun*
tests

A **test** is something you do to show how much you know or what you can do.
Hello Kitty did well in the maths test.

thank *verb*
thanks, thanking, thanked

When you **thank** someone, you tell them that you are pleased about something they have given you or have done for you. You usually do this by saying "Thank you".
My brother thanked me for the birthday present.

theatre *noun*
theatres

A **theatre** is a building where you go to see people acting stories, singing, or dancing.

their

You use **their** to say that something belongs to a group of people, animals, or things.
*They took off **their** coats.*

theirs

You use **theirs** to say that something belongs to a group of people, animals, or things.
*The house next to **theirs** was empty.*

then

1   **Then** means at that time.
    *He wasn't as rich **then** as he is now.*

2   You also use **then** to say that one thing happens after another.
    *Hello Kitty washed her face, **then** went outside to play.*

there

1   You use **there** to say that something is in a place or is happening, or to make someone notice it.
    ***There** are flowers on the table.*

2   **There** also means to a place, or at a place.
    *Hello Kitty has never been **there** before.*

there's

There's is short for **there is**.
***There's** nothing in the box.*

they

You use **they** when you are talking about more than one person, animal, or thing.
***They** are all in the same class.*

they'd

1   **They'd** is short for **they had**.
2   **They'd** is also short for **they would**.
    *The boys said **they'd** come back later.*

they'll

They'll is short for **they will**.
***They'll** be here on Monday.*

they're

They're is short for **they are**.
***They're** going to the circus.*

they've

They've is short for **they have**.
***They've** gone away.*

thick *adjective*
thicker, thickest

1   If something is **thick**, it is deep or wide between one side and the other.
    *He cut a **thick** slice of bread.*

2   If a liquid is **thick**, it flows slowly.
    *This soup is very **thick**.*

thigh *noun*
thighs

Your **thighs** are the parts of your legs that are above your knees.
*Her **thighs** ached from climbing the hill.*

thin *adjective*
thinner, thinnest

1   If something is **thin**, it is narrow between one side and the other.
    *The book is printed on very **thin** paper.*

2   If a person or animal is **thin**, they are not fat and they do not weigh much.
    *He was a tall, **thin** man.*

thing *noun*
things

A **thing** is something that is not a plant, an animal, or a human being.
*What's that **thing** lying in the road?*

think *verb*
thinks, thinking, thought

1   If you **think** something, you believe that it is true.
    *Hello Kitty **thinks** it's a great idea.*

2   When you **think**, you use your mind.
    *Hello Kitty tried to **think** what to do.*

thirsty *adjective*
thirstier, thirstiest

If you are **thirsty**, you want to drink something.

thought
💜 Look at **think**
Hello Kitty thought they were here.

thread *noun*
threads

Thread is a long, thin piece of cotton or wool that you use to sew cloth.

three *noun*
Three is the number **3**.

threw
💜 Look at **throw**
Hello Kitty threw her coat on to a chair.

throat *noun*
throats

1 Your **throat** is the back part of your mouth that you use to swallow and to breathe.

2 Your **throat** is also the front part of your neck.

through
Through means going all the way from one side of something to the other side.
*Hello Kitty walked **through** the forest.*

throw *verb*
throws, throwing, threw, thrown

When you **throw** something you are holding, you move your hand quickly and let the thing go, so that it moves through the air.
Throw the ball to me.

thumb *noun*
thumbs

Your **thumb** is the short, thick finger on the side of your hand.
*The baby sucked its **thumb**.*

thunder *noun*
Thunder is the loud noise that you sometimes hear from the sky when there is a storm.

Thursday *noun*
Thursdays

Thursday is the day after Wednesday and before Friday.
*Hello Kitty saw her on **Thursday**.*

tidy *adjective*
tidier, tidiest

Something that is **tidy** is neat, with everything in its proper place.

A B C D E F G H I J K L M N O P Q R S T U V W X Y Z

tie *verb*
ties, tying, tied

If you **tie** something, you fasten it with string or a rope.
*He **tied** the dog to the fence.*

tie *noun*
ties

A **tie** is a long, narrow piece of cloth that you tie a knot in and wear around your neck with a shirt.

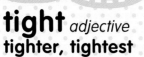

tiger *noun*
tigers

A **tiger** is a large wild cat that has orange fur with black stripes.

tight *adjective*
tighter, tightest

1   If clothes are **tight**, they are so small that they fit very close to your body.
*His trousers were very **tight**.*

2   Something that is **tight** is fastened so that it is not easy to move it.
*The string was tied in a **tight** knot.*

time *noun*

1   **Time** is how long something takes to happen. We measure **time** in minutes, hours, days, weeks, months, and years.
*I've known him for a long **time**.*

2   The **time** is a moment in the day that you describe in hours and minutes.
*"What **time** is it?" — "Ten past five."*

tin *noun*
tins

1   **Tin** is a kind of soft, pale grey metal.

2   A **tin** is a metal container for food.
*She opened a **tin** of beans.*

tiny *adjective*
tinier, tiniest

If something is **tiny**, it is very small.
*Our new kitten is **tiny**.*

tired *adjective*

If you are **tired**, you need to rest or get some sleep.

toad *noun*
toads

A **toad** is a small animal that looks like a frog. **Toads** have rough, dry skin and live on land.

today

Today means the day that is happening now.
*Hello Kitty feels much better **today**.*

toe *noun*
toes

Your **toes** are the five parts at the end of each foot.
*I'm sorry I stood on your **toes**.*

together

If people do something **together**, they do it with each other.
*We played football **together**.*

told

♥ Look at **tell**
*The teacher **told** us the answer.*

tomato *noun*
tomatoes

A **tomato** is a soft red fruit with a lot of juice.

tomorrow

Tomorrow is the day after today.
I'll see you tomorrow.

tongue *noun*
tongues

Your **tongue** is the soft part inside your mouth that moves when you eat or talk.

tonight

Tonight is the evening or night that will come at the end of today.
Hello Kitty is going out tonight.

too

1 **Too** means also.
   Can I come too?

2 You also use **too** to mean more than you want or need.
   The TV is too loud.

took

🖤 Look at **take**
It took me hours.

tool *noun*
tools

A **tool** is something that you hold in your hands and use to do a job.

tooth *noun*
teeth

1 Your **teeth** are the hard, white things in your mouth that you use to bite and chew food.
   You should clean your teeth twice a day.

2 The **teeth** of a comb, a saw, or a zip are the parts that are in a row along its edge.

top *noun*
tops

1 The **top** of something is the highest part of it.
   Hello Kitty climbed to the top of the hill.

2 The **top** of something is also the part that fits over the end of it.
   Hello Kitty took the top off the jar.

tore

🖤 Look at **tear**
Hello Kitty tore her dress on a nail.

torn

🖤 Look at **tear**
Hello Kitty has torn the cover of her book.

tortoise *noun*
tortoises

A **tortoise** is an animal with a hard shell on its back. It can pull its head and legs inside the shell. **Tortoises** move very slowly.

touch *verb*
touches, touching, touched

1 If you **touch** something, you put your fingers or your hand on it.
   The baby touched my face.

2 If one thing **touches** another, they are so close that there is no space between them.
   Her feet touched the floor.

a b c d e f g h i j k l m n o p q r s ❋ **t** u v w x y z ❋

A
B
C
D
E
F
G
H
I
J
K
L
M
N
O
P
Q
R
S
T
U
V
W
X
Y
Z

towards

Towards means in the direction of something.
*Hello Kitty moved **towards** the door.*

towel *noun*
towels

A **towel** is a piece of thick, soft cloth that you use to get yourself dry.

town *noun*
towns

A **town** is a place with a lot of streets, buildings, and shops, where people live and work.

toy *noun*
toys

A **toy** is something that you play with.

tractor *noun*
tractors

A **tractor** is a vehicle with big wheels at the back. **Tractors** are used on a farm to pull machines and other heavy things.

traffic *noun*

Traffic is all the vehicles that are on a road at the same time.
*There is a lot of **traffic** in the town today.*

train *noun*
trains

A **train** is a long vehicle that is pulled by an engine along a railway line.

travel *verb*
travels, travelling, travelled

When you **travel**, you go from one place to another.
*He **travelled** to many different countries.*

tree *noun*
trees

A **tree** is a very tall plant with branches, leaves, and a hard main part that is called a trunk.

triangle *noun*
triangles

1 A **triangle** is a shape with three straight sides.

2 A **triangle** is also an instrument made of metal in the shape of a **triangle** that you hit with a stick to make music.

trick *verb*
tricks, tricking, tricked

If someone **tricks** you, they make you believe something that is not true so that you will do what they want.
*They **tricked** her into giving them money.*

tried

♥ Look at **try**
*Hello Kitty **tried** her best.*

tries

💜 Look at **try**
*Hello Kitty **tries** to help.*

trip *noun*
trips

When you go on a **trip**, you travel to a place and then come back.
*Hello Kitty went on a **trip** to the park.*

trousers *noun*

Trousers are things that you can wear. They cover the part of your body below the waist, and each leg.
Daniel is wearing red trousers.

truck *noun*
trucks

A **truck** is a large vehicle that is used to carry things.

true *adjective*

1 If a story is **true**, it really happened.
   *Everything she said was **true**.*

2 If something is **true**, it is right or correct.
   *Is it **true** that you have six cats?*

trunk *noun*
trunks

1 A **trunk** is the thick stem of a tree. The branches and roots grow from the **trunk**.

2 An elephant's **trunk** is its long nose. Elephants use their **trunks** to suck up water and to lift things.

3 A **trunk** is also a large, strong box that you use to keep things in.

try *verb*
tries, trying, tried

1 If you **try** to do something, you do it as well as you can.
   *I will **try** to come tomorrow.*

2 If you **try** something, you test it to see what it is like or how it works.
   *Would you like to **try** my new bike?*

tube *noun*
tubes

1 A **tube** is a long, round, hollow piece of metal, rubber, or plastic.
   *The liquid goes through the **tube** into the bottle.*

2 A **tube** is also a soft metal or plastic container that you press to make what is in it come out.
   *He bought a **tube** of glue.*

Tuesday *noun*
Tuesdays

Tuesday is the day after Monday and before Wednesday.
*Hello Kitty came home on **Tuesday**.*

tune *noun*
tunes

A **tune** is a piece of music that is nice to listen to.
*She played a short **tune** on the piano.*

tunnel *noun*
tunnels

A **tunnel** is a long hole that goes below the ground or through a hill.

turn *verb*
turns, turning, turned

1 When you **turn**, you move in a different direction.
Hello Kitty turned and walked away.

2 When something **turns**, it moves around in a circle.
The wheels turned slowly.

3 If one thing **turns** into another thing, it becomes that thing.
The tadpole turned into a frog.

4 When you **turn** a machine on, you make it start working. When you **turn** it off, you make it stop working.
Hello Kitty turned off the television.

tusk *noun*
tusks

An elephant's **tusks** are the two very long, curved teeth that it has beside its trunk.

TV *noun*
TVs

TV is short for **television**.
What's on TV?

twelve *noun*

Twelve is the number **12**.

twice

If something happens **twice**, it happens two times.
Hello Kitty has met him twice.

twig *noun*
twigs

A **twig** is a very small, thin branch that grows on a tree or a bush.

twin *noun*
twins

If two people are **twins**, they have the same parents and they were born on the same day. **Twins** often look alike.

twist *verb*
twists, twisting, twisted

If you **twist** something, you turn one end of it in one direction while you hold the other end or turn it in the opposite direction.
Hello Kitty twisted the towel in her hands.

two *noun*

Two is the number **2**.

tying

💜 Look at **tie**
He was tying the two pieces of rope together.

type *noun*
types

A **type** of something is the kind of thing that it is.
Owls are a type of bird.

type *verb*
types, typing, typed

If you **type** something, you write it with a machine, for example a computer.
Hello Kitty typed her name.

tyre *noun*
tyres

A **tyre** is a thick circle made of strong rubber that goes round a wheel. **Tyres** usually have air inside them.

Uu

ugly *adjective*
uglier, ugliest

If something is **ugly**, it is not nice to look at.
*The monster had an **ugly** face.*

umbrella *noun*
umbrellas

An **umbrella** is a long stick that is joined to a cover made of cloth or plastic. You hold an **umbrella** over your head so that you will not get wet in the rain.

uncle *noun*
uncles

Your **uncle** is the brother of your mother or father, or the husband of your aunt.

understand *verb*
understands, understanding, understood

If you **understand** something, you know what it means or why or how it happens.
*I didn't **understand** what he said.*

underwear *noun*

Your **underwear** is the name for the clothes that you wear next to your skin, under all your other clothes.

undress *verb*
undresses, undressing, undressed

When you **undress**, you take off your clothes.

uniform *noun*
uniforms

A **uniform** is a special set of clothes that some people wear to show what job they do, or some children wear to show what school they go to.
*Hello Kitty put on her school **uniform**.*

until

If something happens **until** a time, it happens before that time and then stops at that time.
*Wait here **until** I come back.*

unusual *adjective*

If something is **unusual**, it does not happen very often.
*It is **unusual** for Hello Kitty to be late.*

up

When something moves **up**, it moves from a lower place to a higher place.
*Hello Kitty ran **up** the stairs.*

upon

Upon means the same as **on**.
*Hello Kitty stood **upon** the bridge.*

a b c d e f g h i j k l m n o p q r s t **u** v w x y z

upset *adjective*

If you are **upset**, you are sad because something bad has happened.
Hello Kitty was upset.

upside down

1 If something is **upside down**, the part that is usually at the bottom is at the top.
The picture was upside down.

2 If you hang **upside down**, your head is below your feet.

urgent *adjective*

If something is **urgent**, it is very important and you need to do something about it quickly.
This problem is urgent.

use *verb*
uses, using, used

If you **use** something, you do something with it.
Use a cloth to clean the table.

useful *adjective*

If something is **useful**, you can use it to do something or to help you in some way.

usual *adjective*

Something that is **usual** is what happens most often.
Hello Kitty arrived at her usual time.

usually

If something **usually** happens, it is the thing that happens most often.
Hello Kitty usually takes the bus to school.

valley *noun*
valleys

A **valley** is a low area of land between hills.

valuable *adjective*

If something is **valuable**, it is worth a lot of money.

van *noun*
vans

A **van** is a covered vehicle larger than a car but smaller than a lorry. People use **vans** for carrying things.

vase *noun*
vases

A **vase** is a jar for flowers.

vegetable *noun*
vegetables

Vegetables are plants that you can cook and eat.

vehicle *noun*
vehicles

A **vehicle** is a machine that carries people or things from one place to another.

N.Y.C. TAXI
K T

146

verb *noun*
verbs

A **verb** is a word like 'sing,' 'feel,' or 'eat' that you use for saying what someone or something does.

very

Very is used before a word to make it stronger. *Hello Kitty has a **very** pretty new dress.*

vet *noun*
vets

A **vet** is a doctor for animals.

video *noun*
videos

A **video** is a copy of a film or television programme.

village *noun*
villages

A **village** is a small town.

voice *noun*
voices

Your **voice** is the sound that comes from your mouth when you talk or sing.

volcano *noun*
volcanoes

A **volcano** is a mountain that throws out hot, liquid rock and fire.

vote *verb*
votes, voting, voted

When a group of people **vote**, everybody shows what they want to do, usually by writing on a piece of paper or by putting their hands up. *We **voted** to send money to people who were in the earthquake.*

Ww

waist *noun*
waists

Your **waist** is the middle part of your body.

wait *verb*
waits, waiting, waited

When you **wait** for something or someone, you spend time doing very little, before something happens.

wake *verb*
wakes, waking, woke, woken

When you **wake** up, you stop sleeping.

walk *verb*
walks, walking, walked

When you **walk**, you move along by putting one foot in front of the other.

wall *noun*
walls

A **wall** is one of the sides of a building or a room.

want *verb*
wants, wanting, wanted

If you **want** something, you would like to have it.

A B C D E F G H I J K L M N O P Q R S T U V W X Y Z

war *noun*
wars

A **war** is when countries or groups fight each other.

wardrobe *noun*
wardrobes

A **wardrobe** is a tall cupboard that you can hang your clothes in.

warm *adjective*
warmer, warmest

Something that is **warm** is not cold, but not hot. *The bread is still **warm** from the oven.*

warn *verb*
warns, warning, warned

If you **warn** someone about a possible problem or danger, you tell them about it. *I **warned** them not to go.*

was

♥ Look at **be**
*It **was** Hello Kitty's birthday yesterday.*

wash *verb*
washes, washing, washed

If you **wash** something, you clean it using soap and water.

wasn't

Wasn't is short for **was not**. *Hello Kitty **wasn't** hungry.*

wasp *noun*
wasps

A **wasp** is an insect with wings and yellow and black stripes across its body. **Wasps** can sting people.

waste *verb*
wastes, wasting, wasted

If you **waste** time, money, or energy, you use too much of it on something that is not important. *It's important not to **waste** water.*

watch *verb*
watches, watching, watched

If you **watch** something, you look at it for a period of time.

watch *noun*
watches

A **watch** is a small clock that you wear on your wrist.

water *noun*

Water is a clear liquid that has no colour, taste or smell. It falls from clouds as rain.

wave *noun*
waves

Waves on the surface of the sea are the parts that move up and down. *The **waves** broke over the rocks.*

wave *verb*
waves, waving, waved

If you **wave** your hand, you move it fromside to side, usually to say hello or goodbye.

wax *noun*

Wax is a soft material that melts when you make it hot. It is used to make crayons and candles.

way *noun*
ways

1 A **way** of doing something is how you do it.
*This is the **way** to throw the ball.*

2 The **way** to a place is how you get there.
*We're going the wrong **way**!*

weak *adjective*
weaker, weakest

If someone or something is **weak**, they are not strong.
*When she spoke, her voice was **weak**.*

wear *verb*
wears, wearing, wore, worn

When you **wear** clothes, shoes or glasses, you have them on your body.
*What are you going to **wear** today?*

weather *noun*

The **weather** is what it is like outside, for example if it is raining or sunny.
*What will the **weather** be like tomorrow?*

web *noun*
webs

1 The **Web** is made up of a very large number of websites all joined together. You can use it anywhere in the world to search for information.

2 A **web** is the thin net made by a spider from a string that comes out of its body.

website *noun*
websites

A **website** is a place on the internet that gives you information.
*Hello Kitty's school has a **website**.*

we'd

1 **We'd** is short for **we had**.
We'd left early in the morning.

2 **We'd** is also short for **we would**.
We'd like you to come with us.

wedding
noun
weddings

A **wedding** is when two people get married.

Wednesday *noun*
Wednesdays

Wednesday is the day after Tuesday and before Thursday.

week *noun*
weeks

A **week** is a period of seven days.
*This is the last **week** of Hello Kitty's holidays.*

weekend *noun*
weekends

The **weekend** is the days at the end of the week, when you do not go to school or work.

weigh *verb*
weighs, weighing, weighed

If you **weigh** something or someone, you measure how heavy they are.
*I **weigh** more than my brother.*

a b c d e f g h i j k l m n o p q r s t u v **w** x y z

weight *noun*

The **weight** of a person or thing is how heavy they are.
*What is your **weight** and height?*

well
better, best

If you do something **well**, you do it in a good way.
*She did **well** in her exams.*

well *noun*

A **well** is a deep hole in the ground from which people take water, oil or gas.

we'll

We'll is short for **we will**.
We'll come along later.

went

♥ Look at **go**
*Hello Kitty **went** to school.*

were

♥ Look at **be**
*They **were** at home yesterday.*

we're

We're is short for **we are**.
We're late!

weren't

Weren't is short for **were not**.
*They **weren't** at school yesterday.*

west *noun*

The **west** is the direction ahead of you when you are looking towards the place where the sun goes down.

wet *adjective*
wetter, wettest

If something is **wet**, it is covered in water.

we've

We've is short for **we have**.
We've got lots of books.

whale *noun*
whales

Whales are very large sea mammals.
Whales breathe through a hole on the top of their heads.

what

You use **what** in questions when you ask for information.
What time is it?

wheat *noun*

Wheat is a crop. People make flour and bread from **wheat**.

wheel *noun*
wheels

Wheels are round and they turn. Bikes and cars move along on **wheels**.

wheelchair *noun*
wheelchairs

A **wheelchair** is a chair with wheels that you use if you cannot walk.

when

You use **when** to ask what time something happened or will happen.
When is Hello Kitty leaving?

where

You use **where** to ask questions about the place something is in.
Where is Hello Kitty's house?

which

You use **which** when you want help to choose between things.
Which shoes should I put on?

while

If one thing happens **while** another thing is happening, the two things are happening at the same time.
She goes to work while her children are at school.

whisper *verb*
whispers, whispering, whispered

When you **whisper**, you speak in a very quiet voice.
Don't you know it's rude to whisper?

whistle *verb*
whistles, whistling, whistled

When you **whistle**, you make sounds like music by blowing hard.

white *noun*

White is the colour of snow or milk.
Hello Kitty's skirt is white.

who

You use **who** in questions when you ask about someone's name.
Who won the quiz?

who'd

Who'd is short for **who would**.
Who'd like to come with me?

whole *adjective*

The **whole** of something is all of it.
The boy ate the whole cake.

who'll

Who'll is short for **who will**.
Who'll go and find Mary?

whose

You use **whose** to ask who something belongs to.
Whose bag is this?

why

You use **why** when you are asking about the reason for something.
Why did you do it?

wide *adjective*
wider, widest

Something that is **wide** is a large distance from one side to the other.
The bed is too wide for this room.

width *noun*

The **width** of something is the distance from one side to another.
Measure the full width of the table.

wife *noun*
wives

A man's **wife** is the woman he is married to.

a b c d e f g h i j k l m n o p q r s t u v **w** x y z

A B C D E F G H I J K L M N O P Q R S T U V W ❀ X Y Z

wild *adjective*
wilder, wildest

Wild animals or plants live or grow in nature, and people do not take care of them.

will *verb*

You use **will** to talk about things that are going to happen in the future.
*Mum **will** be angry.*

win *verb*
wins, winning, won

If you **win**, you do better than everyone.
*Hello Kitty has **won** first prize!*

wind *noun*

Wind is air that moves.

wind *verb*
winds, winding, wound

1 If a road or river **winds**, it twists and turns.
2 When you **wind** something long around something, you wrap it around several times.
*She **wound** the rope around her waist.*

window *noun*
windows

A **window** is a space in the wall of a building or in the side of a vehicle that has glass in it.

wing *noun*
wings

The **wings** of birds, insects or aeroplanes are the parts that keep them in the air.

winner *noun*
winners

The **winner** of a race or competition is the person who wins it.
*Our teacher will give the prizes to the **winners**.*

winter *noun*
winters

Winter is the season after autumn and before spring. In the **winter** the weather is usually cold.

wipe *verb*
wipes, wiping, wiped

If you **wipe** dirt or liquid from something, you remove it using a cloth or your hands.
*She **wiped** the tears from her eyes.*

wire *noun*
wires

A **wire** is a long thin piece of metal.
*The birds were sitting on a telephone **wire**.*

wise *adjective*
wiser, wisest

A **wise** person can decide on the right thing to do.

wish *verb*
wishes, wishing, wished

If you **wish** something, you would like it to be true.
*I **wish** I had a pet.*

witch *noun*
witches

In children's stories, a **witch** is a woman who has magic powers that she uses to do bad things.

with

1 If one person is **with** another, they are together in one place.
   *Hello Kitty watched a film **with** her friends.*

2 You use **with** to say that someone has something.
   *My daughter is the girl **with** brown hair.*

without

If you do something **without** someone, they are not in the same place as you are, or they are not doing the same thing as you.
*He went **without** me.*

wives

💜 Look at **wife**
*The men bought flowers for their **wives**.*

wizard *noun*
wizards

In children's stories, a **wizard** is a man who has magic powers.

woke

💜 Look at **wake**
*Hello Kitty **woke** early.*

woken

💜 Look at **wake**
*Hello Kitty was **woken** by a loud noise.*

wolf *noun*
wolves

A **wolf** is a wild animal that looks like a large dog.

woman *noun*
women

A **woman** is an adult female person.

won

💜 Look at **win**
*Hello Kitty **won** first prize.*

won't

Won't is short for **will not**.
*Hello Kitty **won't** be late.*

wood *noun*
woods

1 **Wood** is the hard material that trees are made of.

2 A **wood** is a large area of trees growing near each other.

wool *noun*

Wool is a material made from the fur of sheep. It is used for making things such as clothes.

word *noun*
words

Words are things that you say or write.
*Some **words** are short and some are long.*

wore

💜 Look at **wear**
*Hello Kitty **wore** a red dress.*

work *verb*
works, working, worked

1 When you **work**, you do something that uses a lot of your time or effort.
   *We **work** hard all day.*

2 If a machine **works**, it does its job.
   *The TV isn't **working**.*

a b c d e f g h i j k l m n o p q r s t u v **w** x y z

world noun
worlds

The **world** is the Earth, the planet we live on.

worm noun
worms

A **worm** is a small animal with a long thin body, no bones, and no legs.

worn

♥ Look at **wear**
Have you worn this?

worry verb
worries, worrying, worried

If you **worry**, you keep thinking about problems that you have or about nasty things that might happen.

worse

If something is **worse** than another thing, it is not as good.
My spelling is worse than yours.

worst

If something is the **worst**, all other things are better.
That was the worst day in my life.

worth

If something is **worth** a sum of money, that's how much you could sell it for.
This gold ring is worth a lot of money.

would verb

You use **would** to say that someone agreed to do something. You use **would not** to say that they refused to do something.
Hello Kitty would love to come to the party.

wound

♥ Look at **wind**
She wound the rope around her wrist.

wrap verb
wraps, wrapping, wrapped

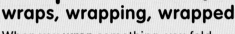

When you **wrap** something, you fold paper or cloth around it to cover it.
Hello Kitty didn't have enough paper to wrap the present.

wrinkle noun
wrinkles

Wrinkles are lines that appear on your face as you grow old.

wrist noun
wrists

Your **wrist** is the part of your body between your arm and your hand. Your **wrists** bend when you move your hands.

write verb
writes, writing, wrote, written

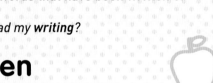

When you **write** something, you use a pen or pencil to make letters, words, or numbers.
Hello Kitty wrote her name in the book.

writing noun

Writing is words that have been written or printed.
Can you read my writing?

written

♥ Look at **write**
My uncle has written a song.

wrong adjective

1 If you say that an answer is **wrong**, you mean that it is not right.
   No, you've got that wrong!

2 If you say that something someone does is **wrong**, you mean that it is bad.
   It is wrong to hurt animals.

A
B
C
D
E
F
G
H
I
J
K
L
M
N
O
P
Q
R
S
T
U
V
W
X
Y
Z

Xx

xylophone *noun*
xylophones

A **xylophone** is an instrument made of flat pieces of wood or metal in a row. You hit the pieces with a stick to make different sounds.

X-ray *noun*
X-rays

An **X-ray** is a picture of the inside of someone's body.
The X-ray showed that my arm was broken.

yacht *noun*
yachts

A **yacht** is a large boat with sails or an engine, used for races or for making trips.

yawn *verb*
yawns, yawning, yawned

If you **yawn**, you open your mouth very wide and breathe in more air than usual because you are tired or bored.

year *noun*
years

A **year** is a period of twelve months, beginning on January 1 and finishing on December 31.

yell *verb*
yells, yelling, yelled

If you **yell**, you shout something, often because you are angry.
She yelled at him to stop.

yellow *noun*

Yellow is the colour of lemons.
Her favourite colour is yellow.

yes

You say **yes** to agree with someone or to say that something is true, or if you want something.

yesterday

Yesterday is the day before today.
There was no school yesterday.

yogurt or yoghurt *noun*
yogurts or yoghurts

Yogurt is a thick liquid food that is made from milk.
Hello Kitty likes strawberry yogurt.

yolk *noun*
yolks

The **yolk** of an egg is the yellow part.

you

You means the person or people that someone is talking or writing to.
Can I help you?

you'd

1 **You'd** is short for **you had**.
I thought you'd told him.

2 **You'd** is also short for **you would**.
You'd like it a lot.

you'll

You'll is short for **you will**.
You'll be late!

young *adjective*
younger, youngest

A **young** person, animal, or plant has not lived for very long.
Tammy is a young monkey.

your

You use **your** to show that something belongs to the people that you are talking to.
I do like your name.

you're

You're is short for **you are**.
You're very early!

yours

Yours refers to something belonging to the people that you are talking to.
His hair is longer than yours.

yourself
yourselves

Yourself means you alone.
You'll hurt yourself.

you've

You've is short for **you have**.
You've got very long legs.

Zz

zebra *noun*
zebras

A **zebra** is a wild African animal like a horse with black and white stripes.

zero *noun*
zeros or zeroes

Zero is the number **0**.

zip *noun*
zips

A **zip** is two long rows of little teeth and a piece that slides along them. You pull this to open or close the **zip**.

zoo *noun*
zoos

A **zoo** is a place where live animals are kept so that people can look at them.